JEWISH BELIEFS AND ISSUES

Michael Keene

Badger Publishing

Badger Publishing Limited
15 Wedgwood Gate
Pin Green Industrial Estate
Stevenage, Hertfordshire SG1 4SU
Telephone: 01438 356907
Fax: 01438 747015
www.badger-publishing.co.uk
enquiries@badger-publishing.co.uk

Badger KS3 Religious Education
Jewish Beliefs and Issues

First published 2007
ISBN 978-1-84691-085-2

Text © Michael Keene 2007
Complete work © Badger Publishing Limited 2007

Acknowledgements
Photos © Alex Keene, The Walking Camera, with the following exceptions:

2 Father and child © Israel Images; 30 Operation Solomon © Denis Cameron;
32 Robert Winston © Ian Bradshaw; 33 Life-support © Shout / **Rex Features**.

10 Settlers © Popperfoto; 16 Chuppah, 25 Pushkes © Israel Images;
31 Israeli Army © PeerPoint / **Alamy**.

18 Elderly, 21 Sabbath, 23 Family © EMPICS.

22 Everlasting Light © Sonia Halliday Photos.

26 Tzedek © www.tzedek.org.uk.

28 Tree-planting © AFP / Getty Images.

Publisher: David Jamieson
Editor: Paul Martin
Designer: Adam Wilmott
Cover photo: Alex Keene
Illustrator: Juliet Breese

Printed in Hong Kong through Colorcraft Ltd.

CONTENTS

WHO ARE THE JEWS?

You will find out

- The name 'Jew' and where it comes from.

- About the faith that Jews share.

In the glossary

Abraham

Ark

Israel

Menorah

Monotheist

Moses

Sabbath Day

Star of David

Synagogue

Torah

In recent years, the Star of David has been adopted as the universal symbol of Judaism.

The roots of the Jewish faith go back a very long way – well over 4,000 years.

During this time, the Jews:

- Have had their own homeland – **Israel** – but have spent hundreds of years as refugees without a home.
- Were slaves for over 400 years in Egypt during the time of **Moses**.
- Were slaughtered in their millions during the 1930s and 1940s.
- Returned to live in Israel in 1948 after an absence of almost 2,000 years.

Today, there are Jewish communities, large and small, in most parts of the world.

WHAT'S IN A NAME?

To understand the world Jewish community, it is helpful to think of it as one very large 'family'. The members of the Jewish family belong to one of the oldest religions in the world. They have not, however, always been known by this name.

1. In the beginning, Jews were known as 'Israelites', from their ancestor, Jacob, who was also known as Israel.

2. Following this, the Jews were called 'Hebrews' after the nomadic tribe of which they formed a part.

3. The word 'Jew' comes from 'Judah', the name of one of the twelve tribes descended from Jacob.

The early names of 'Hebrews' and 'Israelites' have been very important to the Jews because:

- The Jewish scriptures are written in the Hebrew language and most synagogue services are conducted in this language.
- Israel was the name given to the land which God promised to the Israelites after they escaped from slavery in Egypt almost 4,000 years ago. This land was originally known as Canaan but the Jews looked upon it as their Promised Land.

TEN BASIC FACTS ABOUT JUDAISM

1. Judaism began more than 3,000 years ago in Mesopotamia, the region in the Middle East that is modern Iraq.

2. Jews trace their ancestry back to **Abraham**, the father of their nation, and to Moses, who gave them their faith.

3. There are about thirteen million Jews in the world today.

4. Jews worship one God. This means that, along with Christians and Muslims, Jews are **monotheists**.

5. Jews worship in a **synagogue**.

6. The **Torah** is the most important part of the Jewish scriptures.

7. The scrolls of the Torah, the most precious objects in a synagogue, are kept in the **Ark** - a cupboard at the front of a synagogue.

8. The **Sabbath day**, the seventh day of the week, is a day of rest for all Jews.

9. The best-known Jewish symbols are the six-pointed **Star of David** and the seven-branched candlestick [the **menorah**].

10. Jews have their own calendar, which goes back to the traditional date for the creation of the world. This calendar is 3,761 years ahead of the Western calendar.

The seven-branched candlestick is one of the most important symbols of Judaism.

If you were to ask me what it is that makes me feel most Jewish, I would say it's when I am with my family in the home. This is much more important to me than the time I spend in the synagogue. In my home, I am surrounded by many reminders that I am a Jew – and proud of it.

Joseph, 15

OVER TO **YOU** ▶▶▶

1 Explain the three different names that the Jews have been given and the different reasons for them.

2 What is:
   a) Hebrew?
   b) Israel?

3 Read the comment by Joseph. He explains why he is proud to be Jewish. Put his comment into your own words

WHAT DOES IT MEAN TO BE A JEW?

You will find out

- What 'secular Jews' are.

- What it means to be Jewish.

- The links between Jews in the past and Jews today.

In the glossary

Abraham

Bar Mitzvah

Brit Milah

Gentile

Israel

Pesach

Prophet

Rosh Hashanah

Sabbath Day

Secular Jew

Shavuot

Synagogue

Torah

In Israel, a person is recognised as a Jew if he or she has a Jewish mother. In other countries, however, someone is a member of the Jewish community if either of their parents is Jewish. Being born into a Jewish family gives a person a special link with other Jews – including those who are long since dead.

It is now over 4,000 years since God first spoke to Abraham and the Jewish faith began. Since that happened, the Jews have believed that they belong to a very special religious faith.

WHAT DOES IT MEAN TO BE JEWISH?

For most Jews, being Jewish means:

- Believing in the one God who created the heavens and the earth. God made himself known to the world through many **prophets**.

- Keeping the strict food laws and creating a Jewish home.

- Celebrating the Jewish festivals, including **Pesach**, **Rosh Hashanah** and **Shavuot**.

- Celebrating different Jewish ceremonies, extending from a person's birth through to their death. These include **Brit Milah** and **Bar Mitzvah** [Unit 15].

- Sharing in the worship and community life of the local synagogue.

I was born a Jew and I can never lose that. I am very proud of my Jewish heritage. You could argue that Jewish people have given more to the world than any other group. I do not, however, follow any of the Jewish religious practices or festivals.

Ehud, 28

Almost all Jews are born into the faith.

This stained-glass window commemorates the most important of all Jewish festivals – Pesach or Passover.

SECULAR JEWS

Today, there are many Jews who do not follow the traditional practices of their religious faith. In particular, they do not:

- Celebrate the religious festivals.

- Observe the Sabbath day.

- Attend worship in the synagogue.

- Follow the special Jewish laws about food and diet.

These people are called Secular Jews. Secular Jews cannot, however, turn their backs entirely on their Jewish heritage since they still have Jewish parents.

THE JEWISH 'FAMILY'

A non-Jewish person is called a **Gentile**. He or she may have been converted to the Jewish faith but this is highly unusual. Jews do not try to convert other people. The vast majority of Jews were born into the faith. As a result, there is a close link between the Jews of the past and those who are alive today. Jews speak of 'our father, Abraham'.

It is this close link that has led people to talk of the 'Jewish family'. As you will discover in this book, the Jewish faith is all about living in the present. To be a Jew today means following a clear way of life that has not changed in the last 4,000 years. This way of life is laid down clearly in the Jewish scriptures and especially the Torah.

I was born into a Jewish family and my faith has always been very important to me. I try to live my life by following the principles that I find in the Jewish scriptures. I married a Jewish man and we try to bring up our children to respect the traditions and the practices of our faith.

Elizabeth, 32

TAKE TIME TO THINK

Jews throughout the world come from many different backgrounds. What do you think it is that really binds them together into one 'family'?

OVER TO **YOU** ▶▶▶

1 Read through the comments by Ehud and Elizabeth.

   a) What name is used to describe Ehud and what does it mean?

   b) What reason does Ehud give for his pride in being Jewish – although he does not follow the religious practices of the faith?

   c) How does Elizabeth try to put her religious faith into practice?

2 Imagine that you are a Jew. Someone asks you to explain what being Jewish means to you. What answer would you give to them?

UNIT 3
GOD

You will find out

- About the Shema.
- About the Shekinah.
- The story of Rabbi Joshua ben Hananiah.

In the glossary

Abraham

Israel

Moses

Rabbi

Shekinah

Shema

Talmud

Tenakh

As a mark of deep respect, a Jew covers his eyes when using God's name in his prayers.

The Jewish scriptures assume from the beginning that God exists. They do not set out to prove His existence. The very first verse, called the **Tenakh**, makes this clear:

A *"In the beginning God created the heavens and the earth."*

Genesis 1.1

God was there before anything else existed. There is no shadow of doubt about this because of:

- The existence of the world that God has made. God alone could have created the universe, the world and all forms of life.
- The history of the Jews and their continued existence to the present time.

Jewish children are taught to respect God from a very young age.

THE SHEMA

Every morning and evening, Jewish people recite the **Shema** [B]. This prayer is taken from the Jewish scriptures and declares the most basic Jewish belief about God – that there is only one God. This God has no rivals and there is no limit to His power. He has created all of the forces of nature and they are all under His control.

B   *"Hear, O Israel! The Lord is our God, the Lord is one! And you shall love the Lord your God with all your heart and with all your soul and with all your might."*

Shema

THE SHEKINAH

God is over all things and yet He is not isolated from the world. He does not simply live in heaven. God is close to everything and everyone that He has made. God is here, there and everywhere. We read in the Jewish scriptures of God speaking to human beings – Abraham and Moses among them. He shared their lives and was sad, upset, happy and loving alongside them.

Jews have a word to describe this closeness of God. It is called the **Shekinah**. It simply means that God is to be found everywhere. There is no place in the universe where God is not found. The **Talmud**, the Jewish holy book, tells us:

C   *"There is no place without the Shekinah."*

SO WHAT DO JEWS BELIEVE ABOUT GOD?

- **God controls the whole universe.** He is far greater than anything or anyone else that exists. He rules over everything.
- **God can be experienced in the whole of nature.** Every living thing reflects God. Human beings are made in the 'image of God'.
- **God shows himself in history.** In the Jewish scriptures, God intervened many times to save his people, the Jews.

TO END, A STORY

A traditional story is told about **Rabbi** Joshua ben Hananiah from the 1st century CE. He was challenged by a powerful ruler of the time:

"I want to see your God," the emperor said to the rabbi.
"You cannot," the rabbi replied.
"But I insist," repeated the ruler.

The rabbi's response was to point up to the blinding light of the noonday sun.

"Look into the sun," he said.
"I cannot," replied the ruler.
"If you cannot look at the sun, which is one of the servants who stands in the presence of the Holy One, praised be He," said the rabbi, "then is it not even more evident that you cannot see God."

OVER TO **YOU** ▶▶▶

1 Jews believe that everything is under the control of God. Do four drawings to illustrate different parts of life that Jews believe to be under the control of God.

2 Look at Extract B carefully:
  a) Learn the words of the Shema off by heart.
  b) The Shema says one very important thing about God. What is it?
  c) Find out two occasions when the saying of the Shema is important as an act of worship.

THE COVENANT

A wedding ring is a universal symbol of an agreement [a covenant] between a man and a woman.

You will find out

- The meaning of a 'covenant'.
- About the covenant between God and the Jews.
- The two sides to the covenant.

In the glossary

Abraham

Exodus

Israel

Moses

Synagogue

Ten Commandments

When two people make a covenant with each other, it means that they enter into a binding agreement. In any agreement, there are duties to be met on both sides. If one of the sides fails to keep the agreement then it can break down.

The relationship between God and the Jews is based upon a covenant. This agreement was first made between God and Abraham. The special relationship which Jews believe they have with God is based on this covenant.

MAKING THE COVENANT

This unique relationship is a covenant in which two groups, God and the Jews, have made promises to each other in the distant past. The Jewish scriptures are full of examples of the Jews failing to keep their side of the covenant. God, however, never ended the agreement. It still exists today.

Although God first made a covenant with Abraham, its terms were not spelled out until much later. This happened when God gave the **Ten Commandments** to Moses on Mount Sinai. They spell out the rules by which God expected the Jews to live as their part of the agreement.

OVER TO YOU ▶▶▶

1 The photograph shows the Ten Commandments, which are displayed at the front of most synagogues. They are in Hebrew and just list the beginning of each Commandment. Read the Commandments for yourself in Exodus 20.1-17.

   If you look carefully, you will see that the Commandments can be divided into two groups – a Jew's obligations to God and a Jew's obligations to his or her fellow Jews. Draw up a table like the one below to illustrate this:

Obligations to God	Obligations to neighbours
1.	1.
2.	2.
3.	3.
4.	4.

2 Find as many examples as you can of these Commandments being kept or broken today. Look at newspapers, television programmes, etc. Discuss with your partner those Commandments which seem to apply to modern life and those which do not.

BOTH SIDES OF THE COVENANT

God's side of the covenant was quite clear. He promised the Jews that He would:

- Be their God.
- Give them a land to call their own.

Although God threatened to abandon His agreement with the Jews on many occasions, He never did so. No matter how much the Jews misbehaved, God always kept His side of the agreement.

God made demands on the Jews, however, which they consistently failed to keep. If He was to be their God then they must dedicate themselves to serve Him and keep His laws. The most important requirement was that the people should not worship any other gods:

A *"You shall have no other gods beside me. You shall not make for yourself a sculptured image… for I, the Lord your God, am a jealous God."*

Exodus 20.3-5

You can read all of the Ten Commandments for yourself in Exodus 20.1-17.

What did this mean in practice for the Jews? It meant that they were always expected to be faithful to God. They would always be different to the other nations because they would follow God's laws.

THE JEWS WERE PUNISHED

There were two very important occasions in Jewish history when the Jews were punished for breaking their side of the covenant:

- In the early days when the Jews spent over 400 years in Egyptian slavery. God eventually led them out of slavery through the most important event in Jewish history – the **Exodus**. It was after this journey, which took many years, that God gave the Jews their own homeland – the land of Israel.
- The later time when the Jews were banished from their homeland by the Romans. This exclusion lasted for some 2,500 years and only ended in 1948, when the Jews were able to return to Israel.

The Ten Commandments on the wall of a synagogue.

THE ASHKENAZIM AND SEPHARDIM TRADITIONS

You will find out

- The Ashkenazim and Sephardim Jewish traditions.
- The differences between the two traditions.
- The places where the main concentrations of Jews are found.

In the glossary

Ashkenazim

Israel

Sephardim

Throughout history, members of the Jewish community have been great travellers – sometimes as traders but often as refugees. Over the centuries, there have been Jewish communities in most parts of the world. The different groups of Jews today owe their differences to these early settlements.

THE TWO MAJOR GROUPS

There are two main Jewish traditions:

- The **Ashkenazim.** These are the Jews from central and eastern Europe. These Jews originally lived in northern France and different German cities along the River Rhine. The name itself is taken from an ancient German tribe. This tradition developed its own language – Yiddish – which is still used by many Jews today and is a mixture of German and Hebrew. Today, most of the Jews living in the USA, Israel and Australia come from the Ashkenazim tradition.

- The **Sephardim.** This tradition comes from the Hebrew word for Spain. These Jews originally came from Spain and Portugal but they fled to other parts of Europe after being expelled from Spain in 1992. This tradition also has its own language – Ladino, which is a mixture of Spanish and Hebrew – but it is rarely used today.

CHECK IT OUT

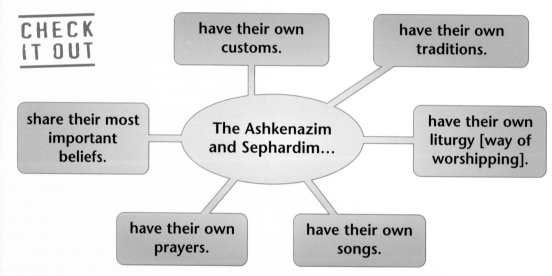

have their own customs.

have their own traditions.

share their most important beliefs.

The Ashkenazim and Sephardim...

have their own liturgy [way of worshipping].

have their own prayers.

have their own songs.

OVER TO YOU ▶▶▶

1. a) What are the two main Jewish traditions?
   b) Write a paragraph to appear in a local paper about these two traditions.
   c) Describe five differences between these two traditions and one thing that they have in common.

2. A young Jew said recently, "You would expect to find most Jews living in Israel but you would be wrong." Was he right? Explain your answer.

This shows where the main numbers of Jews are to be found.

Pie chart:
- Israel 23%
- Russia 14%
- Europe 10%
- Rest of world 8.6%
- South America 3.4%
- North America 41%

DIFFERENCES

The differences between the Ashkenazim and the Sephardim are not ones of beliefs or teachings. They are differences in the words of prayers used; the way of pronouncing Hebrew words; the choice of melodies and chants for public worship and the way in which some customs are carried out.

THE SPREAD OF THE JEWS

Almost all Jews today are descended from the Ashkenazim and Sephardim traditions. The two largest Jewish communities in the world today are found in:

- The USA. There are about 5.5 million American Jews and 2 million of these live in New York alone. A further half million live in Los Angeles.

- Israel. About 4.5 million Jews live in Israel. A small community always lived there but many European Jews moved there in the late 19th and early 20th centuries in response to poverty and persecution elsewhere. Many more Jews arrived after the end of the Second World War [1939-45] and after the founding of the State of Israel [1948].

Among this influx of Jews into Israel were many from Iran and Iraq in the late 1940s and many from Ethiopia in the 1980s and the 1990s. You will find out more about the Jewish community in Ethiopia in unit 30. About 300,000 Jews live in the UK, about 200,000 of them living in London and the south-east of England.

These are the cities in the world where the main concentrations of Jews are to be found.

1,998,000	New York
455,000	Los Angeles
380,000	Paris
335,000	Tel Aviv
298,000	Jerusalem
285,000	Moscow
250,000	Buenos Aires

JEWISH GROUPS

For a very long time, all Jews followed the teachings of the Torah and worshipped in a similar way. The majority still do. They are called **Orthodox Jews**. During the 19th century, however, an increasing number of Jews began to feel differently. They became known as **Reform** or Liberal Jews.

These two groups now exist side by side in Britain and in other countries. In Britain, nine out of every ten Jews belong to the Orthodox tradition.

ORTHODOX JEWS

Orthodox Jews hold very firmly to the teachings of the Torah, or the Law, which was delivered by God to Moses on Mount Sinai.

CHECK IT OUT

Men and women sit separately in the synagogue.

The Hebrew language is used in all services.

Kosher rules about food are kept within the home.

Women cannot be rabbis.

In the Orthodox tradition:

A **Bar Mitzvah** ceremony is held for every boy as he reaches his 13th birthday.

The Sabbath day is kept strictly as a day of rest.

Men wear a **tefillin** as well as a **yarmulke** and a prayer shawl at all weekday services.

In America, most Jews are Conservative Jews. Their beliefs are very similar to those of Orthodox Jews.

REFORM/LIBERAL JEWS

These are Jews who believe that some of the rules in the Torah are out of date.

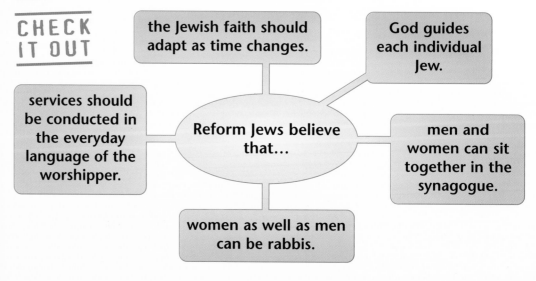

CHECK IT OUT

the Jewish faith should adapt as time changes.

God guides each individual Jew.

services should be conducted in the everyday language of the worshipper.

Reform Jews believe that...

men and women can sit together in the synagogue.

women as well as men can be rabbis.

A large majority of Jews in the UK worship in an Orthodox synagogue.

There are many differences between this Reform synagogue and an Orthodox synagogue.

One of the main reasons why I am a Reform Jew and not an Orthodox one is the way that the two traditions treat women. It cannot be right for men and women to have to sit apart as they worship. Surely a family, a man and a woman, can pray and sing praises to God together?

Rebekah, 23

ORTHODOX AND REFORM JEWS

There are three important differences between Orthodox and Reform Jews:

- **Their attitude towards the Torah is very different.** Orthodox Jews believe that it is God's greatest gift to humankind. It is God's Word and cannot be altered in any way. Reform Jews believe that it was God's Word when it was first given but parts of the Torah no longer apply today.
- **The way in which the Sabbath day is kept is very different.** On this day, Orthodox Jews do not prepare or cook food, use their own cars or light a fire. Reform Jews do not keep these laws.
- **The way that women are treated is different.** In Orthodox synagogues, only men can read the Torah in public or take part in services. In Reform synagogues, women can take part in services.

OVER TO YOU ▶▶▶

1   You can see photographs of two different synagogues – an Orthodox one and a Reform one.

   a)   How might worshippers in these two synagogues prepare for and celebrate the Sabbath day differently?

   b)   In what way will a Jewish boy and a Jewish girl know whether they are being brought up in the Orthodox or Reform tradition?

2   Orthodox and Reform traditions treat women differently. Put yourself in the position of Rebekah from the Reform tradition and discuss her comment.

PATRIARCHS, PROPHETS AND RABBIS

In the distant past, two groups of people – **patriarchs** and prophets – played a very important part in the relationship of Jewish people with God. More recently, their role has been replaced by that of the rabbi.

THE PATRIARCHS

Abraham was brought up in the small town of Ur, in southern Mesopotamia, close to the Persian Gulf. Like everyone else, his family worshipped many gods. Abraham, however, came to believe in the one God who made the heavens and the earth. At about the same time, God promised Abraham that his descendants, the Jews, would be His 'Chosen People'.

Abraham was told by God to travel over 2,000 kilometres to a new country, Canaan. God promised him that the Jews would be a great nation [A]. Abraham and Sarah, his wife, had a son when they were very old. His name was Isaac. Abraham, together with Isaac and his grandson, Jacob, are greatly revered by Jews as the patriarchs [father-figures] of their faith.

A *"I will make you a great nation and I will bless you; I will make your name great, and you will be a blessing. I will bless those who bless you, and whoever curses you I will curse and all the peoples on earth will be blessed through you."*

God's promise to Abraham, Genesis 12.2-3

THE PROPHETS

Long after the last of the patriarchs came the first of the prophets. A prophet was a man or a woman who had been chosen by God to be His messenger, making His will known to the people – someone who spoke on God's behalf.

Although a prophet sometimes spoke about the future, he mainly spoke about those things which greatly displeased God. As many of these evils were committed by kings and religious leaders, it took great courage to speak out about them.

The lives and teachings of the most important prophets were written down and recorded by their disciples. Many of these are kept in the Jewish scriptures, as you will find out in until 11.

THE RABBIS

For a long time, Jewish worship of God was centred on the magnificent **Temple** in Jerusalem. The priests who worked there took over from the prophets as the religious leaders of the community. This stopped, however, when the Temple was finally pulled down, stone by stone, by the Romans in 70CE. The people were dispersed from their homeland and settled in many of the surrounding countries.

Even for these people, however, one part of the old worship remained at the heart of their faith – the Torah. The study of this holiest of all books continued and scholars taught the people about God's Word. These scholars became the first rabbis and they took up the leadership of the Jewish community.

One of the main functions of a Jewish rabbi is to play a prominent part in public worship.

In the last 2,000 years, the part that the rabbi has played in the religious life of a Jewish community has changed little. A rabbi today is expected to have:

- A good knowledge of the Torah.
- A good knowledge of the Jewish law that is based on the Torah.
- A loving and successful home life.

Each country which has a sizeable number of Jews has its own Chief Rabbi. In this country, the Chief Rabbi is always an Orthodox Jew. Each area also has its own **Bet Din** [court], made up of local rabbis. This court has four main tasks:

OVER TO **YOU** ▶▶▶

1 Write a paragraph about:
   a) the patriarchs
   b) the prophets
2 What happened when there were no more prophets and priests?

CHECK IT OUT

Adjudicating in disputes between Jews.

Checking on the instruction of people converting to Judaism.

Four main tasks of the Bet Din

Deciding whether a couple can have a divorce under Jewish law.

Making sure that all food offered as kosher is legitimate.

17

ANTI-SEMITISM AND RACISM

You will find out

- About anti-Semitism.
- The reasons for anti-Semitism.
- About racism and the Jews.

In the glossary

Anti-Semitism

Gospel

Kosher

New Testament

Synagogue

Torah

WHAT IS ANTI-SEMITISM?

For centuries, Jews have found themselves to be the victims of prejudice. This prejudice has a special name – it is called **anti-Semitism**. Anti-Semitism is hatred directed against Jews simply because they are Jews. Jews have often found themselves to be the butt of jokes about their religious traditions, beliefs, ways of worshipping and clothing. In more extreme cases, Jewish graves, kosher shops and synagogues have been defaced, vandalised and attacked.

There have been many examples of anti-Semitism in history:

CHECK IT OUT

1190: massacre of Jews in York.

1290: all Jews expelled from Britain.

1930s: Jews persecuted and slaughtered in Germany.

A few examples of anti-Semitism

11th and 13th centuries: many Jews killed in the Crusades.

14th century: Jews expelled from many European countries.

In the past, Jewish ways of worshipping and their clothing have led to persecution.

THE CHARGES AGAINST JEWS

Why the Jews? For centuries, it was the Christian Church who led the persecution of the Jews. It claimed that:

- **Jews were responsible for the death of Jesus.** This is a charge laid against the Jewish priests in the **Gospels** in the **New Testament**. This is called 'deicide' [God-killing].

- **Jews murdered Christian children and used their blood for their own religious worship.** This false charge, first made in Norwich in 1154, became known as the 'blood libel'.

RACISM

Prejudice is not something that only Jews experience. All groups of people suffer from prejudice at some time – including the disabled, the old, homosexuals and different races. They are picked on because they are, in some way, 'different' and so stand out from others. Prejudice can easily grow into hatred, harassment and violence. Because of their history, Jews have always been strongly opposed to all forms of racism and prejudice. They remember the advice from their scriptures about how foreigners should be treated:

A "*When an alien [a foreigner] lives with you in your land, do not ill-treat him. The alien living with you must be treated as one of your native-born. Love him as yourself, for you were aliens in Egypt. I am the Lord your God.*"

Leviticus 19.33-34

Jews believe that racism is wrong because all people are created and valued by God. They believe that to discriminate against a person is to deny that this person is a part of God's creation. As the Torah says:

B "*God created human beings, making them to be like himself.*"

Genesis 1.27

Jews believe that, if people are made by God, and are like God, then it is quite wrong to hate them. Everyone has been made by God to serve Him in their own, very different, ways. All people must be accepted for what they are.

The teachings of the Torah taught this lesson a very long time ago. Having often been the victims of cruel people themselves, Jews strongly believe that it is wrong to mistreat someone because they are different.

I am a Jew. My friends accept my Jewishness for what it is and it isn't a problem for them. I have not suffered any anti-Semitism myself, although I know of people who have. I have also read in the newspapers and heard on the television of anti-Semitic acts and this worries me a lot. I cannot understand why people cannot leave us alone. Is that too much to ask? Why do people hate the Jews so much?

Anna, 19

TAKE TIME TO THINK

Do you think that your own generation is anti-Semitic in any way?

OVER TO YOU ▶▶▶

In Nazi Germany in the 1930s, fun was often made of Jewish people in public.

1 What is the hatred called that is directed against Jewish people?

2 Why do you think that the Nazis set out to make fun of the Jews before they started to arrest and imprison them?

3 German children were taught in schools to hate the Jews. Why do you think that the Nazis wanted young Jews to be hated by their non-Jewish friends?

THE HOLOCAUST

In the glossary

Gentile

Holocaust

Star of David

Yad Veshem

This statue is one of several erected to remind people of the Holocaust.

The Jews have been one of the most persecuted people in history. This may be because the Jews have always been easily identified as a group – and so open to persecution. It could be because people have always seen them as 'different' – with their own traditions and ways of worshipping.

THE HOLOCAUST

The most serious persecution of the Jews took place in the 1930s-1940s. The Nazis were in power in Germany and their leader, Adolf Hitler, hated the Jews. Stage by stage, Hitler took away all their rights:

CHECK IT OUT

All Jews had to register at a local office.

Jews were not allowed to appear in public unless they wore a badge with the Star of David on it.

A curfew was placed on Jews after 9pm.

Some of the steps taken against Jews in Germany

No German was allowed to buy goods in a Jewish shop.

Jewish children were not allowed to go to school.

No Jew was allowed to own a car or use public transport.

Then the Nazis introduced 'The Final Solution' to the Jewish 'problem'. The intention was to eventually kill all Jews in Germany and those in other countries controlled by Germany.

THE FACTS ABOUT THE HOLOCAUST

The attempt to destroy the Jewish people is called the **Holocaust** [a 'burnt offering']. Between 1935 and 1945:

- Jews were rounded up in vast numbers and shipped off to 28 concentration and death camps.
- The names of these camps became symbols of inhumanity and death – Dachau, Buchenwald, Belsen and Auschwitz. In Auchwitz alone, 6,000 Jews were being gassed each day by 1944.
- Over 6 million Jewish men, women and children were killed altogether in these camps during the Second World War.
- By the end of the Second World War, one in every three Jews in the world had been killed.

THE DIARY OF ANNE FRANK

Anne Frank was a Jewish girl whose family hid from the Nazis in Holland in 1942. Here is a short extract from the diary that she kept:

A *"Countless friends and acquaintances have gone to a terrible fate… the Germans ring at every front door and inquire if there are any Jews living in the house. If there are any, the whole family has to go at once. If they don't find any, they go on to the next house. No one has a chance of evading them unless they go into hiding. Often, they go round with lists and only ring when they know they can get a good haul… In the evening, when it is dark, I often see rows of good, innocent people accompanied by crying children, walking on and on, in charge of a couple of these chaps, bullied and knocked about until they almost drop. No one is spared…"*

Diary entry for 19 November 1942

AFTER THE HOLOCAUST

When the Second World War ended, the world was shocked to discover how many Jews had died. It was strongly felt that such an event must never be allowed to happen again. Regular days of remembrance were set aside.

Yad Veshem, in Jerusalem, is a very special place. The name itself means 'a place and a name'. The 'place' is just a bare room lit by a single candle. The 'names' are those of the different concentration camps inscribed on the floor.

There is another special place at Yad Veshem. It is a line of trees – the Avenue of the Righteous. A tree has been planted for every Gentile who helped a Jew during the war. Many Gentiles lost their lives doing this.

OVER TO YOU ▶▶▶

Dachau, in southern Germany, housed one of the worst concentration camps. It is now a museum and this inscription is found on one of its walls:

PLUS JAMAIS NEVER AGAIN NIE WIEDE NIKOGDA BOLSHE

1 Can you recognise these languages? Why do you think that the inscription is written in these languages?
2 Can you think of three ways in which the rest of the world could make sure that the Holocaust never happens again?

RETURNING HOME

After the Jews rebelled against the Romans in 66CE, they were scattered all over the known world. As a result of this [an event called the **Diaspora**], only a handful of Jews remained in their homeland of Israel – a word that means 'fighter for God'. During the following 1,800 years, most of the people who moved into Israel were Arabs. In fact, by 1900, only one person in ten living in Israel was a Jew.

DRIFTING BACK

Scattered as they were throughout the world, Jewish people rarely found a home. They were looked upon as outsiders wherever they were and treated as such. Despite this, however, most Jews kept their religious faith and traditions. They also retained a deep-seated hope that they would, one day, return to their homeland to live. This belief was called **Zionism**.

Towards the end of the 19th century, more Jews began to drift back to Israel to settle there. Then, in 1917, at the end of the First World War, Arthur Balfour, the British Foreign Secretary, made a very important statement:

A **"***His Majesty's Government views with favour the establishment in Palestine of a national home for the Jewish people… it being clearly understood that nothing shall be done which may prejudice the civil and religious rights of existing non-Jewish communities…***"**

By 1936, one in every three people living in Palestine were Jewish. The Arabs who lived there were greatly alarmed by this. Some of them responded violently but the British gave their support to the Jewish settlers.

THE STATE OF ISRAEL

When the Second World War ended, there was an urgent need to find a home for thousands of Jews who survived the Holocaust. Many who set sail for Israel were turned back by British soldiers. These soldiers found themselves under attack from both Zionists and Arabs.

- The United Nations agreed that Palestine should be divided almost equally between the Arabs and the Jews. The Arabs rejected the proposal.

- The British forces withdrew in 1948.

- The Zionists immediately declared the existence of the State of Israel. The homeland promised by the Jewish prophets of old, such as Amos [B], was once again in Jewish hands.

- The Palestinians, on the other hand, mostly fled the country and remain without a homeland to this day.

B **"***Also I will restore the captivity of My people Israel, And they will rebuild the ruined cities and live in them… And they will not again be rooted out from their land which I have given them.***"**

Amos 9.14,15

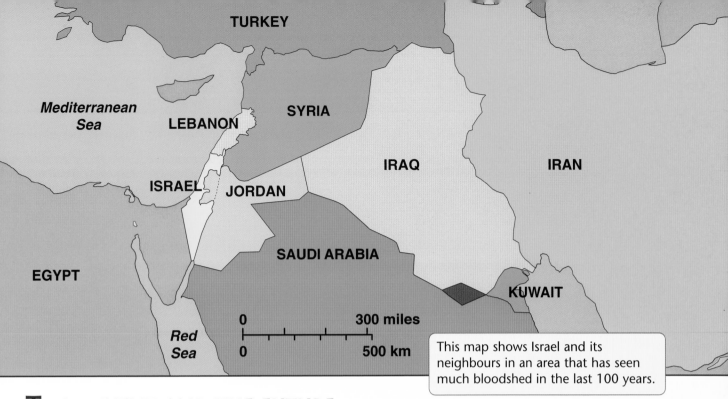

This map shows Israel and its neighbours in an area that has seen much bloodshed in the last 100 years.

THE PRESENT AND THE FUTURE

Yet the new country was far from secure. In 1948 and 1949, a bloody war with Israel's neighbours left over one million Palestinians homeless. Many of them are still without a home. Even today, after four wars in the area [in 1956, 1967, 1973 and 2006], there is still not peace in the area.

This is because:

- The Arabs are still waiting for the Israelis to return land that they have taken in war.

- The Israelis are waiting for the Arabs to recognise that Israel has a right to exist.

Jewish settlers return to live in Israel in 1948.

OVER TO **YOU** ▶▶▶

1 What was the Diaspora?
2 Who were the Zionists and what did they want to achieve?
3 What did Arthur Balfour promise the Jews?
4 How did the Jews eventually achieve a home of their own?

THE JEWISH SCRIPTURES

You will find out

- About the Torah.
- About the Prophets.
- About the Writings.
- About the Talmud.

In the glossary

Ark

Israel

Prophet

Sabbath Day

Sefer Torah

Synagogue

Talmud

Tenakh

Ten Commandments

Torah

Yad

The most important holy book to all Jews is the Tenakh – a popular name for the Jewish scriptures. This document is written in Hebrew and is thousands of years old. There are three parts to it:

THE TORAH

The books of the Torah [meaning 'teaching'] is the part of the Tenakh which Jews value most highly. It contains the first five books of the Bible:

CHECK IT OUT

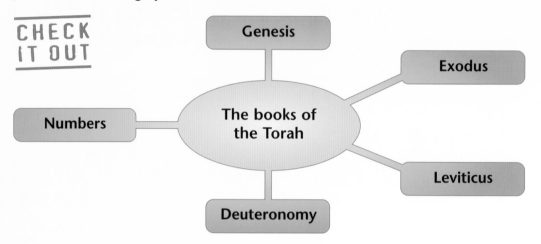

The Torah is valued so highly by Jews because it describes:

- The creation of the universe, the world and all forms of life by God.
- How God chose the Jews to be His special people.
- How God gave the Jews their special laws, including the Ten Commandments.
- How God gave the Jews their homeland – Israel.

The five books of the Torah are written on a single parchment, called the **Sefer Torah**, and kept in the Ark in the synagogue. This is the holiest part of the synagogue and the scrolls are the holiest of all objects. When they reach the end of their life, scrolls are buried and not destroyed.

When the scroll is taken out of the Ark to be read during a service, it is carried above the heads of everyone in the congregation. This is a mark of the respect that is given to it. It is, after all, believed to be the Word of God.

The Torah is divided into 54 sections and one is read on each Sabbath day. Portions are also read on some festival mornings. The person reading from the Torah always follows the passage in the scroll with a **yad** – a metal pointer in the form of a finger – so that no-one's hand actually touches the scroll.

THE PROPHETS

The prophets were the mouthpieces of God and these books were put together by their disciples long after they died. Their writings are among the most beautiful in the Tenakh. There are three longer books – Isaiah, Jeremiah and Ezekiel – and twelve shorter ones. Readings from the Prophets accompany those from the Torah in synagogue services.

The Torah scroll is unrolled in the synagogue.

The yad is used to follow the text in the scroll.

THE WRITINGS

Although the Writings are not so important to Jews as either the Torah or the Prophets, they do contain the Psalms. These are used regularly in synagogue worship and are among the most beautiful in the whole Tenakh. Readings from the Writings are usually given on festival days.

THE TALMUD

For centuries, many opinions and judgements passed down by Jewish teachers built up. They were all to do with the way that Jews were expected to behave.

- These important pieces of information were passed down by word of mouth until, around 200CE, they were collected into one document – the Mishnah.
- People began to discuss the Mishnah and this additional material was included in the Gemara.
- The Mishnah and the Gemara were combined to make the Talmud.

The Talmud, a very large book, still has a great influence on the way that Jewish people live.

OVER TO YOU ▶▶▶

There are several mistakes in this paragraph. Work out what the mistakes are and write out the correct version in your book.

The most important part of the Jewish Bible is the Torah. It contains four books – Genesis, Exodus, Psalms and Deuteronomy. It starts off with the creation of the world and ends with the giving of the Ten Commandments on Mount Ararat. The Torah is divided into 52 units and these are read each day in the mosque but not on Shabbat. Readings from the Writings, such as Isaiah and Jeremiah, are read alongside the Torah.

PRAYER

PRAYER – THE BASIC RULE

Prayer is the most important part of Jewish worship. There is one basic rule about prayer. When Orthodox Jews come together to pray in the synagogue, there must be a minimum of ten males present – a group that is called a **minyan**. This rule has, however, been abolished in Reform synagogues.

DAILY PRAYERS

Jewish synagogues hold three services a day:

- Morning prayer – Abraham prayed early in the morning so that he could meet with God before the business of the day.

- Afternoon prayer – Isaac stopped what he was doing to pray to God in the afternoon.

- Evening prayer – Jacob prayed to God in the evening to thank him for the blessings of the day.

In following this pattern, therefore, Jews are following the example set by the patriarchs.

This man is wearing his prayer shawl for morning prayers.

Jews believe that it is right to cover their head as they enter God's presence.

THE SIDDUR

The **Siddur** is the Jewish prayer book. In the Siddur, prayers have been brought together from many different times and backgrounds. Some of the prayers go back as far as 450BCE. Most of the prayers are in Hebrew, with an English translation.

Synagogue services include many prayers from the Siddur – the most important being the Shema. Three other prayers are also included in all services:

- The Amidah. Eighteen blessings [benedictions] which are at the heart of Jewish worship.

- The Aleynu. A prayer which praises God and prays for Israel and the whole world.

- The Kaddish. A prayer for holiness which is often used when people are in mourning.

A **"***When you pray, do not regard your prayers as a fixed task, but as a plea for mercy and an entreaty before God.***"**

The Talmud

Here are two comments by young Jews about prayer:

> I do not always find time in the day to pray but, when I do, I find it helps me a lot. I prefer to use the old Jewish prayers in the Siddur. Somehow it helps me to know that other people have said the same prayers before me.

Isobel, 20

> I grew up saying my prayers with my parents and my brother. There were times when I found it a real nuisance – especially when I was a teenager. Now, though, I am glad that I picked up the habit. It matters more to me the older I get.

Cavan, 25

SPECIAL CLOTHES FOR PRAYER

Jewish tradition determines that Orthodox men wear certain clothes and objects when they pray:

- The **yarmulke** or skull-cap. Jews believe that the head should be covered by any male entering God's presence.

- The **tallit** or prayer shawl. This is usually made from wool, with black or purple stripes across it, and is worn for morning prayers. At each corner there is an eight-stringed fringe, with a silver or gold fringe at the top.

- The **tefillin**. Very holy objects to all Jewish men, they are two leather boxes which have straps attached. They are wound around the left arm and the forehead to show that the Word of God must enter both the heart and the mind of the person.

TAKE TIME TO THINK

Why do you think that many Jewish parents pray with their children?

OVER TO **YOU** ▶▶▶

1 Look at Extract A.
   a) What does it mean when it says that prayer should not become "a fixed duty"?
   b) What do you think the words 'plea' and 'mercy' mean?
   c) What do you think it means when it says that all prayer should be an "entreaty" before God?

2 Why do you think that Isobel is helped when she feels that she is using words that others have used before her?

FOOD AND DIET

There are strict laws about food and diet in Orthodox Jewish homes – as there are in many religions. The food that Jews are allowed to eat is called kosher. The food which is forbidden to all Jews is called **treifah**. Kashrut is the name given to the different rules which determine whether food is kosher or not.

THE BASIC RULES

The basic laws governing kosher food are set out in the Jewish scriptures in Leviticus 11. These say that acceptable [kosher] food includes:

- Fish that has both fins and scales. This means that Jews are allowed to eat cod and herring but not shellfish and eels.
- Meat from animals that both chew the cud and have cloven hooves are kosher. Meat from sheep, cows and goats is permitted but not any produce from a pig. Jews share this prohibition with Muslims.
- Birds that are bred domestically, like chicken and geese, are kosher but not birds of prey.
- Eggs and milk can be eaten as long as they are taken from animals that are kosher.

KILLING ANIMALS

Jews are only allowed to eat kosher animals if they have been slaughtered by **shechita**. This means that they have been killed by a certified butcher who has followed strict guidelines. Every animal must be killed by passing a very sharp knife across its throat to cut the jugular vein if it is to be kosher. It is claimed that this is the most painless way of killing an animal and the killing of kosher animals must not involve any needless suffering.

The Torah orders that all meat must be free from blood when it is eaten. The carcass, therefore, is hung up after it has been killed until all the blood has drained out. The meat is then soaked in salty water until it is cooked.

SEPARATING MILK AND MEAT

There is a verse in the Torah which says:

A *"You must not cook a young goat in its mother's milk."*

Exodus 23.19

Jewish housewives trying to run a kosher kitchen take this to mean that meat and milk products must not be cooked or eaten together. They must be kept separate at all stages in the preparing, cooking and clearing up process. To achieve this, Jewish housewives keep separate sets of kitchen utensils and saucepans so that the two can be prepared and washed up without coming into contact with each other. After they have eaten meat, Orthodox Jews wait several hours before eating any milk product.

OVER TO YOU ▶▶▶

1 Look at the diagram which shows the food items that Jews may, and may not, eat. Compare the items in the diagram with those mentioned in Deuteronomy 14.3-21.
   a) Make two columns in your book. Put in one column those foodstuffs that are kosher and the other those that are not.
   b) Imagine that you are inviting a Jewish friend round for supper. Plan a menu that would be in keeping with kosher limits. Compare your menu with that of your partner. Discuss your two menus and decide which of you has come up with the most attractive menu.

2 Look at each of these items. Which of them would be considered kosher for a Jew to eat and which would not. Explain your answers.

   a) Beef stroganoff

   b) Prawn salad

   c) Beefburger, egg and chips

   d) Pork sausages

   e) Roast chicken

THE MEZUZAH

The mezuzah is attached to a doorpost. In this way, a portion of God's Word is fixed to almost every room in the house – and the outside as well.

The home is a very special place for all Jews. It is in the home, rather than in the synagogue, that the most important worship of God takes place. Home is the place where Jewish parents teach their children the traditions of their faith. It is also in the home that children learn just what it means to be Jewish.

WHAT IS A MEZUZAH?

Jewish homes display one symbol which announces its Jewishness – the **mezuzah**. This is a small parchment scroll on which is written the most important statement of Jewish belief – the Shema. This begins with the words:

A "*Hear, O Israel! The Lord is our God, the Lord is one.*"

Deuteronomy 6.4

You will find a mezuzah on the doorpost of every room in the house except the bathroom and toilet. There will also be one on the outside of the house itself. Why, though, is the mezuzah there? The Jewish scriptures have the answer:

B "*And these words [the Shema] which I command you this day shall be upon your heart... and you shall write them upon the doorposts of your houses and upon your gates...*"

Deuteronomy 6.9

Some people touch the mezuzah as they go in and out of a house or room.

TAKING CARE OF A MEZUZAH

The scroll in the mezuzah must be handwritten on parchment by a Jewish scribe. The parchment of animal skin must come from a kosher animal. The parchment is then placed within a protective casing before being nailed to the right-hand doorpost, towards the top.

Some Jews wet two fingers on their right hand before touching the mezuzah as they go into a room or leave it. This is a sign of their respect for God and for the Torah – from which the words on the parchment are taken.

As the mezuzah is a holy object, so:

- Care must be taken to keep it in good repair.
- The writing on the parchment must always be legible.
- The case must be opened every three years by a scribe so that it can be checked.
- If necessary, the parchment can be mended or replaced.

A mezuzah is important because of what it symbolises:

CHECK IT OUT

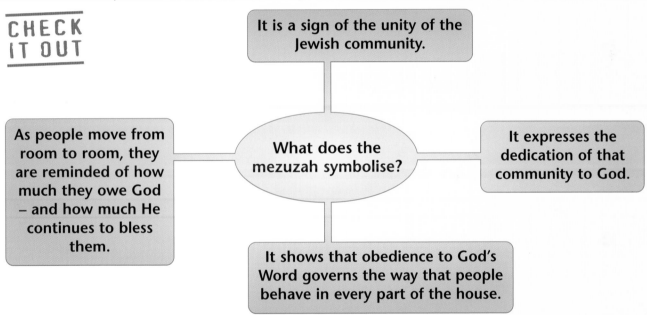

It is a sign of the unity of the Jewish community.

As people move from room to room, they are reminded of how much they owe God – and how much He continues to bless them.

What does the mezuzah symbolise?

It expresses the dedication of that community to God.

It shows that obedience to God's Word governs the way that people behave in every part of the house.

OVER TO YOU ▶▶▶

1   Copy out each of these sentences, putting the correct beginning with the correct ending.

   a) The mezuzah is written on...   the most important statement of Jewish belief.

   b) The Shema is...   must come from a kosher animal.

   c) The skin for a mezuzah...   near the top of a doorpost.

   d) A mezuzah is nailed...   parchment made from animal skin.

   e) By touching a mezuzah...   sometimes needs to be replaced.

   f) The Shema in a mezuzah...   Jews are showing their respect for God.

2   If you were asked to explain to a group of non-Jewish visitors to a synagogue why a mezuzah is very important to Jews, what would you say?

CHILDHOOD

You will find out

- About circumcision.
- About Bar Mitzvah.
- About Bat Mitzvah.

In the glossary

Abraham

Bar Mitzvah

Bat Hayil

Bat Mitzvah

Brit Milah

Circumcision

Mohel

Orthodox Jew

Rabbi

Sabbath Day

Synagogue

Torah

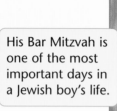

His Bar Mitzvah is one of the most important days in a Jewish boy's life.

Being Jewish affects a person's whole life, from the moment they are born until the time they die. There are Jewish ceremonies or rituals to mark all of the important times in a person's life.

CIRCUMCISION [BRIT MILAH]

The birth of a baby is greeted with great joy in both a Jewish home and the wider Jewish community. Jewish tradition insists that the birth of a baby is the result of co-operation between:

- God
- the mother
- the father

Every child is seen as a gift from God to be loved and cherished.

Circumcision is the oldest of all Jewish practices which are still carried out today. It goes all the way back to Abraham, who was told by God to circumcise all the male members of his family.

A *"God said to Abraham… every male among you shall be circumcised. And you shall be circumcised in the flesh of your foreskin and it shall be a sign of the Covenant between Me and you."*

Genesis 17.9-11

The ceremony, performed on every Jewish boy, must take place on the 8th day after birth – even if that day is the Sabbath. The ceremony, in which the foreskin of a boy's penis is removed, is carried out in the child's home by a **mohel**. The mohel does not need to be a rabbi or a doctor but he is a specially trained religious Jew.

BAR MITZVAH

Bar Mitzvah marks a boy's entry into adulthood. It is held on the first Sabbath day after his 13th birthday, by which time he must have learned to read a passage from the scriptures in Hebrew in the synagogue.

His Bar Mitzvah is a very important event in the life of every Jewish boy. Until now, his father has been held responsible for the boy's religious education but, now, the boy is responsible for his own spiritual welfare. During the service, the father thanks God that he is no longer responsible for his son keeping the Jewish faith [B]. The boy is now an adult and old enough to take life's most important decisions for himself.

B **"**Blessed is the One who has freed me from the responsibility for this child's conduct.**"**

From Bar Mitzvah ceremony

> *I have just celebrated my Bar Mitzvah. I learned Hebrew in our classes at the synagogue – although it is frightening to stand up in front of all your relations and friends to read from the Torah in a language that you do not usually use. I want to be able to keep as many of the Jewish laws as possible, to live a life that is faithful to God and to establish my own Jewish home in the future.*

Joshua, 13

BAT MITZVAH

Jewish girls join adult society a year earlier than boys – after their 12th birthday. In some non-Orthodox synagogues, there is a special ceremony for girls, called **Bat Mitzvah**, in which girls read from the Torah.

In many Orthodox synagogues, there is a ceremony for girls in which, although they do not read publicly from the Torah, they do give a special talk about the Torah reading for that week. This is called the **Bat Hayil** ['the woman of virtue']. If you read Proverbs 31.10-31, you can work out why it has this name.

Many non-Orthodox synagogues hold a Bat Mitzvah ceremony for girls on their 12th birthday.

OVER TO **YOU** ▶▶▶

1 a) Why is the boy in the photograph reading from the Torah?

   b) What preparation has been necessary before this boy is ready to read from the Torah in public?

2 a) His Bar Mitzvah is a very special day in the life of every Jewish boy. Describe a day which has been very special in your life.

   b) Write a paragraph to describe how excited a Jewish boy might be as his Bar Mitzvah draws close. What changes do you think he might notice in his life from this day onwards?

MARRIAGE

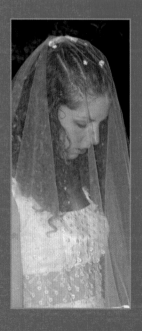

The Talmud says that a man is incomplete without a wife. It advises every Jewish man to study first and then to marry – but, if he cannot wait, then he can reverse the order!

Marriage is very important for all Jews. There is very strong pressure on a Jew to marry another Jew. Jews who marry Gentiles cannot have a Jewish wedding in a synagogue. Such marriages are not encouraged because it is believed that the couple are bound to disagree over the religious upbringing of any children they might have.

AN IMPORTANT EVENT IN THE COMMUNITY

Weddings are very happy and important events in the Jewish community. Marriage is believed to be a gift from God which will bring untold blessings on the couple in the years ahead.

After their marriage, the couple are going to set up a new home together and, God willing, will bring a new generation of Jewish children into the world. This means that they will make a great contribution to the future health of the Jewish faith.

THE JEWISH WEDDING SERVICE

Jewish weddings do not have to take place in a synagogue, although they usually do. They can be held on any day of the week except the Sabbath day and festival days. Its distinctive features are:

- **A period of fasting precedes the wedding.** Both bride and groom seek God's forgiveness for their past sins. This is so that they can start their married lives together without any secrets.

- **The wedding takes place under a special canopy called a chuppah.** The canopy, which has a pole at each corner, symbolises the home that the couple are going to set up together. The chuppah is sometimes decorated with white flowers.

- **The reading of the ketubah – the wedding contract.** This contract pledges that the husband will provide for his wife in case he dies or wishes to divorce her.

- **The seven blessings.** During the service, the groom gives his wife a ring and the rabbi pronounces seven blessings on the couple. These blessings thank God for the creation of the world and for giving such joy and happiness to human beings. The couple share a glass of wine as the blessings are read out.

- **The breaking of a wine glass beneath the groom's foot.** This is a reminder that the old Temple in Jerusalem was destroyed by the Romans centuries ago. It also reminds the couple that they will have some difficult times ahead in their married life as well as many happy times.

- The groom gives his bride a ring and formally takes her in marriage. In Reform synagogues, the couple do this to each other. As the groom gives the ring to his bride, he says:

A *"Behold you are sanctified [made holy] to me with this ring, according to the law of Moses and Israel."*

The service ends with everyone shouting out 'Mazel Tov' [Good luck].

A JEWISH STORY

A traditional Jewish story underlines the belief that, although marriage is very important, it can also be very difficult. A rabbi was asked by a middle-aged Roman woman, who was not a Jew, what the God that Jews believed in had been doing since He created the world. 'Making marriages,' he said to her, 'that is as difficult as dividing the waters of the Red Sea.' To prove the rabbi wrong, the woman took a thousand of her male slaves and a thousand of her female slaves and 'married' them to each other. By the morning, they were all miserable. The woman was forced to admit that it was not easy to make a happy marriage. Only God could do it successfully.

TAKE TIME TO THINK

What do you think is the main point of the story and how is this point underlined in the marriage service?

OVER TO **YOU** ▶▶▶

In the Jewish scriptures, we read that: "When a man takes a new wife, he shall not go out with the army, nor be charged with any duty; he shall be free at home one year and shall give happiness to his wife whom he has taken." [Deuteronomy 24.5]

1 Why do you think that the husband in ancient Israel was given a year free of any duties to spend with his wife?

2 Do you think a similar idea might be a good idea in our society?

A Jewish couple begin their married life by standing together under the chuppah.

In the glossary

Bet Din

Get

Israel

Ketubah

Synagogue

Talmud

Judaism values marriage very highly indeed. If a marriage is beginning to fail then every effort is made to save it. Much of this effort comes from the Bet Din court, which acts as a marriage guidance counselling service. It is only when every effort has failed that divorce proceedings can begin [A].

A *"Whoever divorces his first wife, even the altar sheds tears on his behalf."*

The Talmud

THE DOCUMENT OF DIVORCE

In the Jewish scriptures, only men are allowed to obtain a divorce. The wife does not have to consent to the divorce. He has to obtain a 'letter of divorce' [called a **get**].

When the couple married, steps were taken to protect the wife in the case of a divorce. The ketubah – the marriage document – assured the woman that she would be looked after if her husband divorced her.

The modern get states the exact details of the divorce. The woman must produce this document if she ever wishes to remarry. This is intended to give her some real protection. At the same time, there is a real measure of inequality about the Jewish divorce laws. The system certainly does not treat men and women equally.

Until very recently, a man could divorce his wife and then refuse to give her a get certificate. This meant that she could not remarry if she wanted to. The Jewish community, however, now puts pressure on any man who refuses to grant his wife a get. They are even threatened with expulsion from their synagogue.

THE JEWISH DIVORCE PROCEDURE

1. The two people must agree that they wish to divorce.

2. They must both attend a meeting with the Bet Din court. If this proves impossible then they can send a representative.

3. A scribe writes out a get. The husband then hands the get to his wife in front of two witnesses.

4. The couple are divorced from the moment that the get is handed over.

A woman can ask the Bet Din for a divorce. She can claim that her husband:

- has been unfaithful to her.

- treats her cruelly.

- cannot father children.

The Bet Din may find in her favour but it cannot compel her husband to grant her a divorce.

The ketubah, the wedding document signed by the groom, was intended to guarantee a wife that she would be looked after if her husband ever wanted a divorce.

If both husband and wife agree to a divorce then they become divorced in the eyes of the Jewish community. In Britain, however, they must also go through the ordinary divorce court and be granted a civil divorce. It is only in Israel that a civil divorce is not necessary.

There is one important difference between a religious and a civil divorce. In a civil court, a couple need to produce a reason for a divorce – unfaithfulness or cruelty. The Bet Din court does not require a reason. It is enough that a couple have tried to save their marriage and have failed.

TAKE TIME TO THINK

Many people find it very surprising that, in the past, Jewish men but not Jewish women could obtain a divorce. Do you think that it was enough simply to try to protect women from the hardship that a divorce inevitably caused?

OVER TO YOU ▶▶▶

1 Extract A comes from the Talmud.
   a) This quotation is saying something very important about divorce. What is it?
   b) Is it surprising that the Jewish faith, which lays such an emphasis on family life, should make divorce so easy? There is a reason for this. Try to work out what it is.

2 Imagine that you are a Jewish man or woman. You wish to divorce your husband or wife. Describe, in your own words, the steps that you have to take to make this possible.

CHECK IT OUT

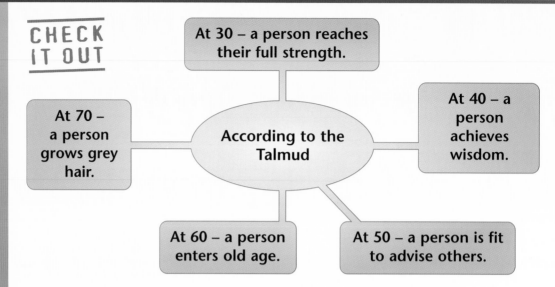

At 30 – a person reaches their full strength.

At 40 – a person achieves wisdom.

At 70 – a person grows grey hair.

According to the Talmud

At 60 – a person enters old age.

At 50 – a person is fit to advise others.

Like other religions, Judaism places a great emphasis on the traditions and customs of the past. The past history of the Jewish people is very important and so needs to be preserved and kept alive. It must be handed down from generation to generation. Older people have a very important part to play in this.

The Jewish religion calls older people 'elders'. The elders in the community bring a great deal of wisdom along with their advice to every situation. This wisdom comes from their long experience of life. The Talmud demands that great care should be taken of the elderly person who has forgotten his or her learning through senility. Young people must learn to accept that elderly people become increasingly frail and make allowances for this.

A *"Rise before a grey-haired person and honour the face of the old."*

Jewish saying

Jewish tradition says that one of the benefits of growing old is that it leaves more time to pray and read the scriptures.

HONOURING PARENTS

There is a mitzvah (commandment) which requires children to honour and fear their parents. Tradition has insisted that the same honour should also be extended to grandparents. In practice, this means:

- not contradicting their point of view or arguing with them.
- not calling them by their first names since this shows a lack of respect.
- not losing your temper with them.
- standing up when they enter the room [A].
- feeding and clothing your parents and grandparents when they can no longer look after themselves.
- speaking respectfully of them after they die.

If a child can no longer look after his or her parents, they must be provided for. It is acceptable for elderly Jewish parents to be looked after in a residential home but only if that is the last resort. A child also has the responsibility of making sure that his or her parents are properly buried and that all funeral expenses are met.

YOUNG PEOPLE AND THE ELDERLY

These two comments were made by young people about the elderly members of their family:

> I often go to my grandmother for help and advice. She seems to bring a lifetime of experience to bear before she even opens her mouth. It is not always easy to explain what I mean. You know when someone is being wise without necessarily being able to explain what you mean.
>
> Elizabeth, 18

> My grandfather is well into his seventies. As a Jew, I have always been taught to respect him and listen to what he has to say. I try to do this but it is not always easy. As a young person, I have some clear ideas of my own – and my grandfather doesn't always agree with me! I still find his ideas worth listening to, though.
>
> David, 17

TAKE TIME TO THINK

Read Elizabeth's and David's comments carefully. How do you think it is possible to recognise wisdom in elderly people? Where do you think that wisdom comes from? What do you think it means to 'honour' and 'respect' the older members of your family? Does it always mean doing what they say?

OVER TO YOU ▶▶▶

1 Why do you think Judaism places such importance on respecting elderly people?

2 What do you think the commandment means when it says that the young should "rise before a grey-haired person"?

3 What do you think it means to "honour the face of the old"? What might it mean in practice to 'honour' those who are old?

DEATH AND BEYOND

You will find out

- What happens when a Jewish person dies.

- The four stages of mourning.

- Jewish beliefs about life after death.

In the glossary

Heaven

Hell

Israel

Messiah

Onan

Synagogue

Talmud

Jews believe that everyone will be judged by God after their life has been weighed in the balance.

All Jews hope that they will be granted the strength to say this prayer before they die:

A. *"My God and the God of my fathers, accept this prayer; do not ignore my supplication. Forgive me all the sins I have committed in my lifetime and may it be your will to heal me. Yet, if you have decreed that I should die... may my death atone for all my sins and transgressions which I have committed before you... Grant me a share in the life to come... into your hands I commend my spirit."*

The Siddur

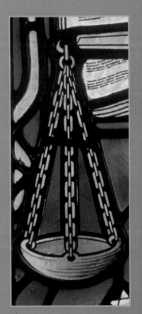

AFTER DEATH

Once a Jewish person has died:

- Their eyes and mouth are closed by a close relative. The body is then washed and wrapped in a single linen shroud and placed in a simple wooden coffin. In death, everyone is treated the same.

- Within 24 hours, burial takes place.

- Working together, the mourners fill the grave with earth. By doing this, they are confirming in their own mind that the person is dead and showing their unity with those who mourn.

The four stages of mourning

- Stage 1. The time between death and the funeral – during this time, the mourner [called the **onan**] is released from every other obligation.

- Stage 2. The week of mourning that follows the funeral – mourners are expected to stay in their own home and sit on the floor on low stools to receive visitors.

- Stage 3. A further period of 23 days during which life gradually returns to normal.

- Stage 4. A period of light mourning which lasts until the end of the 11ᵗʰ month after the person's death.

A memorial or tombstone can be set up any time after the earth has settled on the grave. Some mourners, however, prefer to have a memorial stained-glass window erected to the deceased's memory in their synagogue.

Take Time to Think

Read Extract A carefully. Explain, in your own words, what you think is meant by the words "Yet, if you have decreed that I should die... may my death atone for all my sins and transgressions which I have committed before you."

The afterlife

There is little mention in the Jewish scriptures of a life after death. The Talmud warns against any speculation about a life after death because "no eye has seen it".

Many Jews, however, believe that:

- God rewards the righteous in the life to come.

- God punishes the wicked in the life to come

- God will resurrect all people and bring them back to life.

A person's life, with all their deeds, is weighed in the balance.

The coming of the Messiah

Ever since earliest times, Jews have believed in the coming of the **Messiah**. The Messiah is a superhuman figure sent by God to deliver Israel from all their enemies. He will set up God's kingdom on earth.

This kingdom, however, will not be the end. At the end of the world, the non-Jewish dead will be brought back to life by God and:

- The unrighteous will be judged by God and sent to Gehinnom – hell. **Hell** is not a place of everlasting torment. It lasts for 12 months, during which the unrighteous will be cleansed from their sins. These people will then enter God's presence.

- The righteous will pass straight into **heaven**.

B *"People in this world fulfil commandments and do not know the value of what they have gained. In the world to come they will realise what they have achieved."*

Jewish saying

OVER TO YOU ▶▶▶

1 a) Describe the four stages of mourning that Jews pass through after they have lost a loved one.

   b) Mourning is carefully structured in the Jewish community. How do you think this might help someone who has lost a loved one?

2 Write down a list of four things that Jews believe about life after death.

JUDAISM AND WOMEN

TWO DIFFERENT PICTURES

In the first two chapters of the Jewish scriptures, Genesis 1 and 2, two different pictures are presented:

1. In the first, God created the first man and woman together. They were equal but not the same. They lived together in the Garden of Eden and were equally involved in the first sin – although most of the blame was attached to the woman.

2. In the second, God created the man first. The man was given the task of naming the animals in the garden. He returned to God afterwards to report that none of the animals were his equal. God took pity on the man and created the woman to be his 'helpmeet'. The woman was made from the man's rib. The implication is that she was, in some way, his inferior.

These two pictures are reflected in the different kinds of Jewish communities that exist today.

WOMEN IN ORTHODOX JUDAISM

In Orthodox Judaism, the traditional attitude towards women, based on the second picture, is followed:

CHECK IT OUT

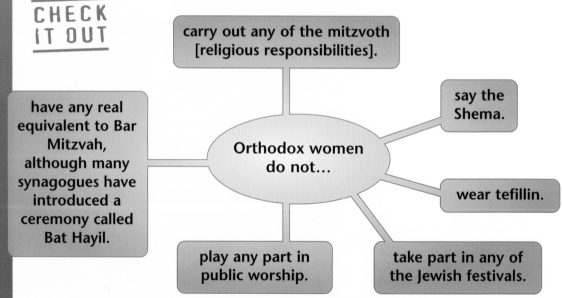

Orthodox women do not...

- carry out any of the mitzvoth [religious responsibilities].
- say the Shema.
- wear tefillin.
- take part in any of the Jewish festivals.
- play any part in public worship.
- have any real equivalent to Bar Mitzvah, although many synagogues have introduced a ceremony called Bat Hayil.

In the past, Orthodox women have not been expected to learn the Torah since their domestic and family responsibilities would have prevented this. Now, however, more women are taking the opportunity to study the Torah and so increase their knowledge of their faith. The importance attached to the education of women and girls has increased considerably.

In this synagogue, men and boys sit in the well of the buildings with women and children in the balcony.

A woman is reading from the Torah scroll.

WOMEN IN REFORM JUDAISM

About one in every ten Jews belong to synagogues in the Reform tradition. These are synagogues which do not place such a high importance on the old Jewish traditions and ways of life. The Torah is important but the old laws do not have to be followed slavishly:

- Jewish girls in Reform synagogues have their own ceremony at the age of 12 called Bat Mitzvah [Daughter of the Covenant]. During this ceremony, a girl can read in public from the Torah – a privilege which in Orthodox synagogues is reserved strictly for men only.

- Women can train to be rabbis. This involves having a large part to play in leading public worship and the teaching that goes on in a synagogue. Women can also be called up to read from the Torah on the Sabbath day – something they are not allowed to do in an Orthodox synagogue.

OVER TO YOU ▶▶▶

1   In the photograph on this page, you can see a woman reading from the Torah in a synagogue service.

a) Is this service being held in an Orthodox or a Reform synagogue – and how can you tell?

b) What other differences might you notice between the two different kinds of service?

2   There are considerable differences in the role of men and women in Orthodox and Reform families. Make a table like the one below and complete it:

Orthodox Judaism		Reform Judaism	
Men	*Women*	*Men*	*Women*
1.			
2.			
3			
4.			

KEEPING THE SABBATH DAY

You will find out

- The two events celebrated every Sabbath day.
- How Jews prepare for the Sabbath day.
- About celebrating the Sabbath day.

In the glossary

Ark

Bimah

Challah

Exodus

Havdalah

Israel

Orthodox Jew

Rabbi

Sabbath Day

Sefer Torah

Synagogue

Torah

This table is laid and ready for the Sabbath meal.

The Sabbath day is the Jewish day of rest and the only weekly Jewish festival. It reminds all Jews of:

- The creation of the world. The Jewish scriptures tell us that God created the world in six days and then rested on the seventh [A]. Jews also rest on the seventh day of the week.
- The delivery of the Israelites from over 400 years of slavery in Egypt. This event [the Exodus] is the most important event in Jewish history.

A   *"For in six days the Lord made the heavens and the earth, the sea and all that is in them, and rested on the seventh day; therefore the Lord blessed the Sabbath day and made it holy."*

Exodus 20.112

PREPARING FOR THE SABBATH DAY

In most Jewish homes, the Sabbath day is different from every other day of the week:

- As no work is allowed on the Sabbath, so all work needs to be done before the Sabbath begins – at sunset on the Friday evening.
- The Sabbath table has to be laid. This is the meal that all of the family share on the Friday evening and is the most important event of the Sabbath day. New cutlery is brought out and laid on the table. The candlesticks are cleaned and wine is placed on the table.
- Each member of the family has a bath and puts on their best clothes. Candles are often lit before the Sabbath day begins to drive away any sorrow and unhappiness.

A VISIT TO THE SYNAGOGUE

The males in the family attend a service in the synagogue at the start of the Sabbath day. In this service, the Sabbath is greeted as a wife would greet her husband. As the service closes, the rabbi drinks a glass of wine and repeats the prayer of holiness. In this, he thanks God for the great gift of the Sabbath day to God's people.

AT HOME

Before the Sabbath meal begins at home, the family drink wine [a symbol of happiness] together. The father then blesses his wife and children – a custom going back to biblical times. In the Sabbath meal, a special loaf of bread [a **challah**] is broken, dipped in salt and eaten. Each course is ended with the singing of a song.

THE SABBATH SERVICE

The family attend the Sabbath service together, although they do not sit together in an Orthodox synagogue. In the service itself:

- The Torah is read. The Torah scrolls are kept in the Ark and, when this is opened, everyone stands up. The scroll to be read, called the Sefer Torah, is taken out and carried to the **bimah**. During a year, the whole of the Torah must be read in public in 54 instalments.
- After the Torah has been read, the rabbi gives his sermon.
- As the people leave the synagogue, they wish each other 'Shabbat Shalom' ['the peace of the Sabbath'].

This Jewish girl is welcoming in Shabbat by lighting a Sabbath candle.

HAVDALAH

The final act of the Sabbath day is the **Havdalah** ['separation'] ceremony. This 'separates' the Sabbath day from the other days of the week. Wine is drunk and a special candle with several wicks is lit, while a spice box is opened to wish everyone a 'sweet-smelling' week ahead.

OVER TO YOU ▶▶▶

1 a) What does the word 'Havdalah' mean?
   b) Why do you think the ceremony at the end of the Sabbath day is given this name?

2 Why do you think a spice box is opened at the end of the Sabbath – and the start of a new week?

CHECK IT OUT

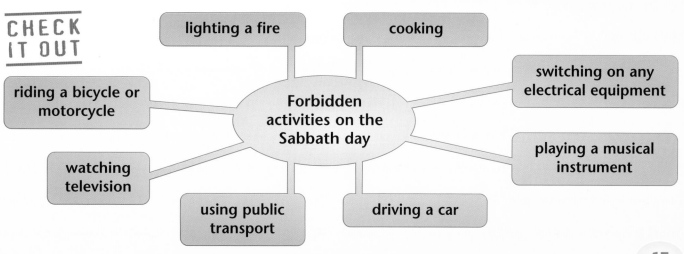

Forbidden activities on the Sabbath day

- lighting a fire
- cooking
- switching on any electrical equipment
- playing a musical instrument
- driving a car
- using public transport
- watching television
- riding a bicycle or motorcycle

THE SYNAGOGUE

The Ark houses the all-important scrolls on which the Torah is written.

INSIDE A SYNAGOGUE

All synagogues are built facing the city of Jerusalem, where Solomon built the first Temple in the 10th century BCE. This city is close to the heart of every Jew.

Step inside a traditional Jewish synagogue and you will find:

- **Separate worship areas for men and women.** The men pray on the lower floor while the women and children sit in the gallery.

- **The Ark, the holiest part of a synagogue.** The Ark is a cupboard at the front of a synagogue which houses the scrolls on which the books of the Torah are written.

- **A raised platform called the bimah.** During a service, the Sefer Torah is carried to this raised platform to be read. As people 'go up' to read, so this shows the people that God's Word, the Torah, is higher than any human being.

THREE IMPORTANT SYMBOLS

Three symbols in the synagogue are also very important:

- The **Everlasting Light** which always burns above the Ark. This light, which burns oil, is never allowed to go out – symbolising the Jewish belief that God is always present with them.

- Two stone or wooden tablets on the wall above the Ark in most synagogues on which the Ten Commandments are written – or at least the beginning of each one. These sayings, at the very heart of the Torah, underline the importance of the Tenakh.

- The six-pointed Star of David, made up of two equilateral triangles. This was an ancient symbol of fire and water. In the Middle Ages, it was regarded as a shield against evil.

USING THE SYNAGOGUE

Synagogues are really 'community centres'. They bring Jews together to:

- **Celebrate.** The most important events in a Jew's life are often held in the synagogue – circumcision, Bar Mitzvah, marriage and funeral celebrations.
- **Learn.** Judaism stresses the importance of learning, from the beginning to the end of life. Children and young people are often taught by the rabbi, and other members, on Sunday mornings.
- **Relax.** Youth clubs, crèches and mother and baby groups together with clubs and societies all use synagogue facilities.
- **Worship.** Every Sabbath day, Jewish men, women and children come to the synagogue to worship God. They also attend special services at the many Jewish festivals.

THE ROLE OF THE RABBI

A rabbi is a person who is well respected in the Jewish community because he or she is trained in the Torah as well as Jewish law and tradition. In Orthodox synagogues, the rabbi is always male but, in Reform synagogues, rabbis can be male or female. The rabbi takes part in Sabbath worship by leading prayers, reading from the Torah and giving a sermon. He or she also conducts weddings, funerals and classes to educate members of the community about their religion, as well as visiting the sick and the bereaved.

OVER TO YOU ▶▶▶

1 Imagine that you are a Jewish person living in an area where there are many other Jews. You join a synagogue that has just opened. You find yourself on a committee which has to make the synagogue as widely known as possible.

   a) Design an advertisement to go into the Jewish Chronicle, advertising the synagogue.

   b) Design a leaflet to be put through the doors of Jewish people in the area, telling them about the many activities that take place in the synagogue.

2 The scrolls of the Torah are the holiest objects in any synagogue. Carry out some research to discover:

   a) How these scrolls are made and what material is used.

   b) What is written on the scrolls.

   c) Who writes and prepares the scrolls.

   d) Where the scrolls are kept in the synagogue.

   e) How a new scroll is presented to the synagogue and what happens to it at the end of its life.

FAMILY LIFE

For Jews, family life is very important. It brings security and love to all family members. It is the place where children receive their first education and where they form their identity. It provides someone to turn to when family members have problems – emotional, financial or health.

The Torah and the rabbis set down basic rules about how families should be run:

HUSBAND AND WIFE

The duty of a husband to his wife is set out in the ketubah – the marriage contract that the groom signs at his wedding. He promises to support his wife:

A *"...even if I have to sell the coat from off my back."*

The ketubah also sets out rules for looking after the wife if her husband divorces her.

THE DUTIES OF PARENTS

In Jewish families, parents and children have responsibilities to each other. Parents must feed and clothe their children and teach them how to live as good Jews. In addition:

CHECK IT OUT

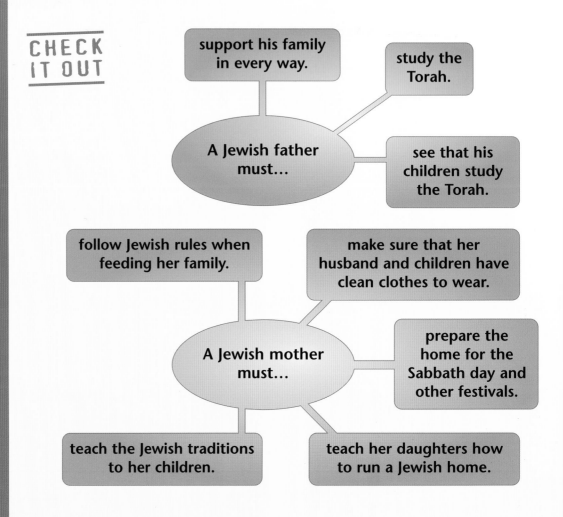

support his family in every way.

study the Torah.

A Jewish father must...

see that his children study the Torah.

follow Jewish rules when feeding her family.

make sure that her husband and children have clean clothes to wear.

A Jewish mother must...

prepare the home for the Sabbath day and other festivals.

teach the Jewish traditions to her children.

teach her daughters how to run a Jewish home.

Judaism lays down some firm rules about how each member of a family is expected to behave.

Parents must also train their children for good jobs and pass on the necessary practical skills. The Talmud warns parents:

B *"Teach your son a trade or you teach him to be a thief."*

The Talmud also says that parents should teach their children basic survival skills. Today, this would include road safety and being careful about talking to strangers. This might sound like simple common sense but, for Jews, it is more than this – it is a religious duty.

THE DUTIES OF CHILDREN

C *"Respect your mother and father so that you may live a long time in the land that I am giving you."*

Exodus 20.12

It is a Jewish religious duty that children should always respect their parents and take care of them. The Talmud says:

D *"See that they eat and drink, and take them where they need to go."*

If parents make mistakes then their children should correct them – but always with tact to avoid hurting their feelings.

A STORY WITH A MORAL

A father once came to Rabbi Israel Baal Shem Tov [1698-1760].

"Rabbi, what shall I do? My son is drifting into evil ways."
"You must love him," replied the rabbi.
"But Rabbi," replied the father, "you don't understand. He lies and cheats. He works on the Sabbath. He even steals."
"In that case," said the rabbi, "you must love him even more."

OVER TO **YOU ▶▶▶**

Work with your partner to:

1 Make a list of five things which, in your opinions, make a happy family.
2 Share your ideas with the rest of the class, listen to their ideas and decide on the most important three items for your final list.

TAKE TIME TO THINK

Read the story about Rabbi Israel Baal Shem Tov and think about it. What do you think the rabbi was trying to teach the father?

WEALTH AND POVERTY

A *"Who is rich? He who is satisfied with what he has."*

Ethics of the Fathers

Jews believe that every year, on Rosh Hashanah [Jewish New Year], God decides how much wealth each person will have. It is, therefore, pointless to try to become richer, since everything is in the hands of God.

WEALTH

Judaism teaches that there is much more to life than simply trying to become rich. At the same time, material possessions are needed if a person is to serve God properly.

B *"Where there is no flour there is no Torah."*

Mishnah

Judaism teaches that the happy man will steer a middle path between striving after wealth and spending his time on other things.

C *"Give me neither poverty nor riches… in case I become too full and say 'Who is God?' or in case I become poor and steal."*

Proverbs 30.8-9

The Torah warns people against the danger of becoming too preoccupied with trying to make as much money as possible. Unless people are very careful, it will lead them away from God.

D *"Take care not to forget the Lord your God… in case when you have eaten and are satisfied and have built fine houses and live in them, and when your herds and flocks increase, and your silver and gold and all that you have has increased, then your heart be lifted up and you forget the Lord your God."*

Deuteronomy 8.11-14

Wealth does not have any real value unless people use it properly.

E *"When a man leaves the world, neither silver nor gold, nor precious stones or pearls, accompany him but only the Torah he has learned and the good works he has carried out."*

Mishnah

Jews are taught that wealth is a gift from God to be shared with the poor.

Jews are required to give money regularly so that the poor can be helped.

POVERTY

The Talmud says that poverty is worse than 50 plagues. His poverty makes the poor person miserable. This places a big responsibility on those who are wealthy.

F   *"There will always be poor people in the land. Therefore I command you to be open-handed towards your brothers and towards the poor and needy in your land."*

Deuteronomy 15.11

All Jews are required to give a **tithe** [one tenth] of their earnings to charity. To keep all of one's wealth to oneself is to rob the poor. Although the poor are excused from paying the tithe, they are expected to give something. In Jewish thinking, everyone is expected to help the poor – including the poor themselves.

Jews are also expected to set aside money for celebrating the Sabbath day and other festivals. Poor Jews often cut down their weekly expenditure to make the Sabbath day special. The family meal on the evening of the Sabbath day is particularly important.

TAKE TIME TO THINK

Why do you think that Jews believe that it is important to encourage the poor to help themselves?

OVER TO YOU ▶▶▶

1   Write down three things that Jews believe about wealth.

2   Write down three things that Jews believe about poverty.

3   "Jews do not believe that poverty is a good thing or that there is any spiritual benefit to be had from being poor." Is the speaker right and does this sum up the Jewish attitude to wealth and poverty?

GIVING TO CHARITY

Judaism teaches that there are two different kinds of charity:

- Giving material gifts such as food and money. To describe this kind of giving, Jews use the word **tzedaka** [righteousness].
- Giving in the form of physical labour or advice.

GIVING TO THE POOR

It is possible to give directly to the person in need but this could cause them real embarrassment. It is better that the giver does not know who is receiving the money – and the receiver does not know who is giving to them. Those who give are encouraged to think of their gift as a loan – a loan that they do not expect to be repaid. At the same time, the receiver can hope that they will be able to repay the loan 'some day'.

The problem with doing this is that, after the loan has been received, and used, the person is left as poor as they were originally.

A Jewish holy man who lived in the 12th century taught that there are actually eight degrees or levels of charity and each one is better than the one before:

1. To give grudgingly.
2. To give cheerfully – but less than one should.
3. To give only when asked.
4. To give before being asked.
5. To give in such a way as the donor and the recipient do not know the other.
6. To give in such a way that the donor knows who receives the gift but the recipient does not know who gave it.
7. To give anonymously.
8. To help people to help themselves by giving them a loan or finding them a job.

Jews put the same principles into operation when they give aid to poor countries. They prefer to look beyond the emergency and give help which allows the poor to help themselves through long-term projects such as building hospitals or schools.

Young Jews often put part of their pocket money into pushkes boxes each week.

GIVING TIME AND ENERGY

Giving one's own time and energy is called gemilut hassadim [good deeds]. There are many ways in which people who are part of a Jewish community try to help those who are in need:

CHECK IT OUT

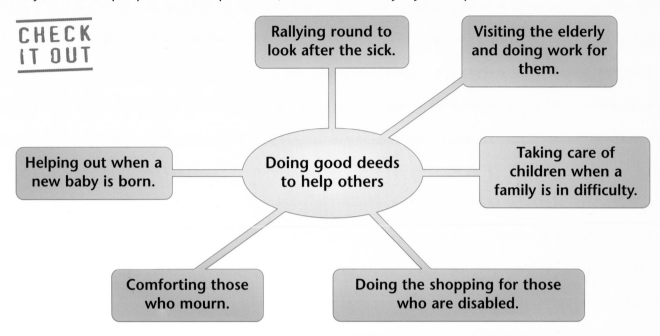

Rallying round to look after the sick.

Visiting the elderly and doing work for them.

Helping out when a new baby is born.

Doing good deeds to help others

Taking care of children when a family is in difficulty.

Comforting those who mourn.

Doing the shopping for those who are disabled.

PUSHKES

You will find **pushkes**, collecting boxes in support of many Jewish charities, in almost every Jewish home. People use them to collect the small change left over after shopping expeditions.

The collecting of money for charity involves Jewish children as well as their parents. Children are encouraged to put part of their weekly pocket money in the pushkes. Children often make their own pushkes and put a few pennies in regularly from an early age. This encourages them to share their wealth with those who are less fortunate.

> *I was brought up in an Orthodox Jewish home. I cannot remember a time when there wasn't a pushkes box in the house. We used to make our own. Each week, I would put some of my pocket money in the box and, when it was full, we would send it off to a charity. I now do exactly the same with my children. It is a good habit to learn.*
>
> Esther, 32

TAKE TIME TO THINK

Do you think that the eight degrees of charity are right? Explain your answer.

OVER TO YOU ▶▶▶

1 a) How important do you think it is to give money to charity?

b) When you have children of your own, will you teach them to give some money away to charity from an early age?

2 Explain what is meant by gamilut hassadim and give some examples.

TWO JEWISH CHARITIES

Here we will look at two Jewish charities which take a similar approach to creating a fairer and more just world. First, though, a verse from the Jewish scriptures to set the scene:

A *"He has showed you, O man, what is good. And what does the LORD require of you but to do justice, and to love kindness and to walk humbly with your God."*

Micah 6.8

WORLD JEWISH RELIEF

Since its creation 70 years ago, World Jewish Relief has been committed to saving individuals and Jewish communities wherever in the world the need is greatest. Its basic work is sending volunteers to countries such as China, South Africa, the Ukraine and Argentina to work for 3-6 months.

The volunteers take food, clothing, medicine and training to people who are disadvantaged, with two purposes in mind:

- **To help those in need.** Short-term help is provided but also more long-term programmes are also begun and local people are trained to take over when the volunteers leave.

- **To help those who volunteer.** There is a strong emphasis on the volunteers building up strong relationships with local people to increase their understanding of those living in different countries with cultures very different to their own.

One recent example of the work of World Jewish Relief has been in China. For a very long time, China has been a closed country, but one way of helping it in the future is to build up its tourism. This will be particularly important when the Olympic Games are held in Beijing in 2008. A volunteer has been put in place to work with local people encouraging Jewish people to visit China.

CHECK IT OUT

strong organisational skills.

strong communication skills.

experience of working among young adults.

The ideal candidate for Beijing has:

Jewish knowledge.

experience of living in a foreign country.

experience of working in a Jewish community.

a reasonable level of computer literacy.

You can find out more about the work of World Jewish Relief by visiting www.worldjewishrelief.org.uk/projects.

These volunteers are working on one of many Tzedek projects.

TZEDEK

- Tzedek comes from the Hebrew word meaning 'justice'. The Jewish organisation of this name believes that the Jewish way of dealing with injustice in the world is to help the poor help themselves. Tzedek concentrates on small projects in the poorest parts of the world.

- The areas in which Tzedek is active include Africa, Asia and Latin America. It sends volunteers to the poorest countries to work alongside local people on various health projects – concentrating on the prevention of HIV/AIDS. It knows only too well that many young children have been turned into orphans through the death of one or both parents from the disease and it works to provide shelters, hostels and homes for them.

- Set up in 1990, Tzedek also works on smaller projects which are intended to help people set up their own businesses and be able to build their own hospitals and schools.

- At the same time, Tzedek knows that it can only expect support from Jews at home if it educates them about world poverty. This is a very important part of Tzedek's work. There are special boxes in most Jewish homes to encourage people to give for the work. These are particularly important in the task of interesting children and young people in its work.

You can find out more about the work of Tzedek by visiting www.tzedek.org.uk.

TAKE TIME TO THINK

What do you think that volunteers might be able to take to a country like China and what do you think the country might give to them?

OVER TO YOU ▶▶▶

Describe the work that:
a) World Jewish Relief
b) Tzedek
does to make the world a fairer place.

CREATION AND THE GARDEN OF EDEN

You will find out

- About the six 'days' of creation.
- The teaching of the creation account.
- About the Fall.

In the glossary

Rabbi

Here we pick up on the Jewish concern for the environment. This concern is rooted very firmly in the two accounts of the creation of the world in the Jewish scriptures:

ACCOUNT 1 [GENESIS 1]

This account takes us through the six 'days' of creation:

CHECK IT OUT

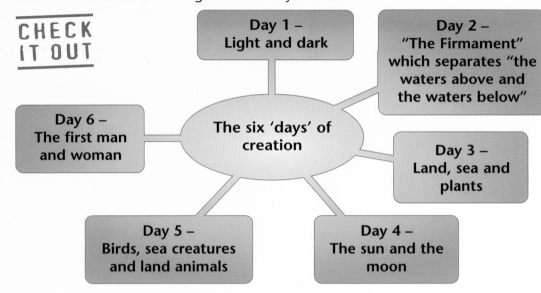

The six 'days' of creation

- Day 1 – Light and dark
- Day 2 – "The Firmament" which separates "the waters above and the waters below"
- Day 3 – Land, sea and plants
- Day 4 – The sun and the moon
- Day 5 – Birds, sea creatures and land animals
- Day 6 – The first man and woman

A *"In the beginning, when God created the universe, the earth was formless and desolate. The raging ocean that covered everything was engulfed in total darkness..."*

Genesis 1.1

Jewish rabbis have long pointed out that, in this description, God is frequently said to have looked at his own handiwork and "saw that it was good". God then rested on the seventh day.

ACCOUNT 2 [GENESIS 2]

This account concentrates on the creation of the first man, Adam, and the first woman, Eve. We are told that it was God's will to make both the male and the female so that they could support each other and begin populating the earth.

Most Jews believe that these are not descriptions of actual events but are religious 'myths'. As such, they teach important 'truths' about God and His purpose for the world.

In particular, they teach that:
- God created the world, although we do not know how this was done.
- God had a purpose in creating the universe, the world and all life. The beginning of life was not an accident – it was a deliberate act of God. God was very satisfied with his work.
- Human beings are different from all other forms of life. They are the only ones said to be created 'in the image of God'. Jews believe that human beings alone have a 'spirit' or a 'soul'. They alone can worship and serve God.
- Human beings have been given responsibility by God to look after His creation.

You will find out more about this in unit 28.

THE FALL

There is another very important part to the story of creation – in Genesis 3. When God created the first man and woman, they were placed in a perfect garden, the Garden of Eden. They didn't even need to work to obtain their food – it was ready at hand. God only put one restriction on the two of them:

B   *"Then the Lord God placed the man in the Garden of Eden to cultivate it and guard it. He said to him, 'You may eat the fruit of any tree in the garden, except the tree that gives the knowledge of what is good and what is bad. You must not eat the fruit of that tree; if you do you will die that same day...'"*

Genesis 2.15-17

TAKE TIME TO THINK

If you read Genesis 3, you will find out what happened next in the story. The story of the Fall may be a myth but do you think it is also saying something important about human nature?

The Jewish scriptures hold Eve responsible for the Fall. She encouraged Adam to disobey God.

OVER TO YOU ▶▶▶

1 Describe two differences between the two accounts of creation in the Jewish scriptures.

2 Why do you think that Jews call the description of Adam and Eve disobeying God the 'Fall'?

3 Describe in your own words the account of the Fall in the Jewish scriptures.

JEWS AND THE ENVIRONMENT

You will find out

- The Jewish attitude to looking after the world.

- The Jewish attitude to conservation.

- The Jewish attitude to pollution.

In the glossary

Israel

Sabbath Day

Talmud

Torah

A *"The earth, and everything in it, is the Lord's."*

Psalm 24.1

As we saw in unit 27, the Torah teaches that God created a world that was perfect for human beings to live in. All that human beings are expected to do is to look after this world.

DO NOT DESTROY GOD'S WORLD

Both the Torah and the Talmud give guidelines for treating the planet properly. One of the most important principles is that nothing should be destroyed unnecessarily.

B *"When you lay siege to a city… you must not destroy its trees by taking an axe against them… for the tree of the field is man's life…"*

Deuteronomy 20.19

In biblical times, an army attacking a city would lay siege to it by building a wall around it so that no one could enter or leave. Jews were commanded not to cut down fruit trees for the siege walls. This was taken to be a command that nothing should be destroyed during the conflict.

Every tree that is uprooted in Israel must be replaced.

CONSERVATION

Jews believe that everything should be carefully conserved. To do this, an area of open land was kept around each town – called a migrash. No one could grow crops or operate a business there. It provided an area where people could walk as well as limiting the size of the town. In biblical times, all towns had a migrash.

Jews also enhanced the beauty of their countryside by planting a circle of fruit trees around each town. Since 1948, the planting of trees has always been a priority in Israel since it prevents soil erosion and helps to remove pollutants from the atmosphere. The Jewish National Fund was originally set up to buy land to put these principles into practice but it now funds many conservation projects under the slogan 'Working for a greener Israel'.

Find out all that you can about the Jewish National Fund by looking at www.brijnet.org.

POLLUTION

Jewish teaching makes these very important points about the environment:

- All human beings must work to control pollution by recycling waste and not wasting energy. This promotes human well-being and improves human health.

- The Talmud teaches that businesses that cause annoyance or produce harmful substances should be kept well away from humans. Such businesses must put in place a safe means of destroying waste products before they start.

- Human beings are much more important than any other part of creation. The Jewish scriptures speak of them being 'stewards' appointed by God to look after creation. They must look after the whole of creation – including the animal world.

THE SABBATH RULE

Land for which Jews were responsible was allowed to rest, lie fallow, for one year in every seven. This reflected the Sabbath custom which stipulated that all human beings, and animals, should cease all work for one day in every seven. Land must rest if it is going to be productive.

It is interesting that these Sabbath day regulations also covered not just human beings but slaves and animals as well. All of the rules reflected the statement in the account of creation that God 'rested' after spending six days creating the world.

A FINAL STORY

There is an old Jewish story that tells how Adam was very depressed after he was thrown out of the Garden of Eden. He believed that he would have to search for food like every other animal. God, however, told him that he would have the privilege of working for his food. Adam revived. He knew that this would make him different to any other animal.

OVER TO YOU ▶▶▶

1 a) What is migrash?
   b) What is the link between migrash and looking after God's creation?

2 a) Do you think that farmers today could allow their land to lie fallow for one year out of seven?
   b) Do you think the land would really benefit if they did?

3 What would you say to someone who said, "I didn't ask to be born. I can treat the world as I like because I will be dead before the earth really suffers"?

JEWS AND CARING FOR ANIMALS

A *"A righteous man pays attention to the needs of his animals."*

Proverbs 12.10

In its opening chapter, the Torah describes the creation of animals:

B *"Then God said, 'Let the water team with swarms of living creatures and let birds fly above the earth...' and God made the animals according to their kinds, the beasts according to their kinds and all the things that creep on the earth."*

Genesis 1.20

It then describes how God created humans to have "control over the fish of the sea and the birds of the sky, over the animals and over the whole earth". [Genesis 1.26]

Jews take two important lessons from these verses:

- Animals are God's creatures and must be treated as such.
- Animal life can never have the same value as human life.

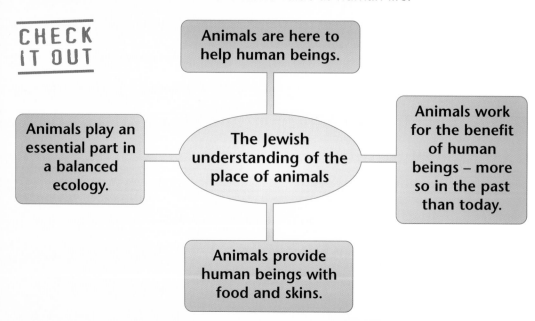

CHECK IT OUT

Animals are here to help human beings.

Animals work for the benefit of human beings – more so in the past than today.

Animals play an essential part in a balanced ecology.

The Jewish understanding of the place of animals

Animals provide human beings with food and skins.

There were certain rules in Jewish society that put these principles into practice. So:

- Human beings rested on the Sabbath day so that their beasts of burden could also rest.
- At harvest time, the horse or ox pulling a wagon was not to be muzzled, so that it could help itself to the produce as a reward.
- A farmer was not allowed to have an ox and an ass pull the plough at the same time because they had unequal strength.
- If a person wanted to take eggs from a bird's nest they must first shoo the mother bird away.

Jewish people always try to be kind to animals without suggesting that they are as important as humans. Jews intensely dislike any cruelty to animals.

Animals and their welfare are a very important part of the Jewish understanding of God's world.

ANIMALS FOR FOOD

There is nothing in the Jewish scriptures which tells Jews to eat meat. There is nothing to stop them becoming vegetarians if they wish. At the same time, Jews are not recommended to follow a vegetarian way of life.

However, the scriptures do teach that, if animals are killed for food, then they must be slaughtered as painlessly as possible. For Jews this is called shechita.

EXPERIMENTS ON ANIMALS

Over three million scientific experiments are carried out on animals in the UK every year. Jews insist on two points when looking at this:

- Inflicting unnecessary pain on an animal is strictly forbidden.
- If such experiments improve the life of human beings, then it is justified. If not, there is no justification for it.

These two principles would rule out the use of animals to improve such things as cosmetics. Finding cures for diseases, however, is extremely important and will be supported by Jews.

OVER TO YOU ▶▶▶

1 How do you think that thinking of animals as part of God's creation might influence the way that a person treats them.

2 You read a report in a newspaper of animal rights activists releasing animals that are being bred to use in scientific experiments. A Jewish person writes a letter to the editor of the local paper giving their opinion of this. Write that letter.

TAKE TIME TO THINK

The Jewish scriptures state that human beings have 'control' over animals. What do you think this really means? What is allowed and what is ruled out?

OPERATION SOLOMON

Many Jews left Ethiopia for Israel during Operation Solomon.

AN ISOLATED JEWISH COMMUNITY

For centuries, a community of up to 50,000 Jews lived in the northern province of Gondar in Ethiopia. This is a very poor area and this community was isolated from Jews in the other parts of the world. The community called itself 'Beta Israel' – the 'house of Israel'.

In the 17th century, Beta Israel fought for its independence from Christian Ethiopia but without any success. It was only in the 19th century that the Beta Israel community began to forge links with Jews in other countries. In the 1970s, anti-Semitism became an increasing problem in Gondar and many Jews wanted to leave the area and settle in Israel – their homeland. The Ethiopian government refused to give them the necessary permission.

PERMISSION TO LEAVE

Terrible famines in Ethiopia in the 1970s led Israel to mount several 'rescue' operations to bring out the Ethiopian Jews. In 1984 and 1985, almost 8,000 of them were rescued and brought to Israel. In the following five years, more Jews were taken from Ethiopia but many had to be left behind – mainly the elderly, women and children. They either could not travel or could not be resettled in a new home.

By 1990, there was such unrest in the country that many countries were very worried about what might happen to the Jewish community in Gondar. On Friday, May 24th 1991, the rebels fighting the government of Ethiopia began to close in and threaten everyone standing in their way. This is when Operation Solomon was put in place.

TAKE TIME TO THINK

Many of the Jews taken from Ethiopia to Israel have found it very difficult to settle into their new home. Imagine that you are one of these Jews. In what ways do you think you might have found it very difficult to settle into Israel?

OPERATION SOLOMON

In just 36 hours, 14,325 Ethiopian Jews were taken out of the country and given entry to Israel. 34 El-Al Hercules C-130 aircraft, with the seats removed so that they could carry as many passengers as possible, flew non-stop until all of those given permission to leave had reached Israel.

In Operation Solomon, twice as many Jews were taken to Israel as those transported in two other operations – Operation Moses and Operation Joshua – around the same time.

There are still, however, over 20,000 Jews left in Ethiopia and these are in some danger. They suffer from a lack of basic necessities and medical care. It seems that it will be a long time before these people are able to join their relatives and friends in Israel.

At the same time, the 36,000 Ethiopian Jews who are living in Israel live a very basic life without many of the facilities that other people take for granted. This is an often forgotten group. Since it left Ethiopia, it has faced many problems in becoming adjusted to life in Israel. Some people from outside Israel send money to help it meet medical bills and school supplies.

OVER TO YOU ▶▶▶

1 What was the size of the Jewish community in Gondar, Ethiopia?

2 What did the community call itself and what did the name mean?

3 Why did the community want to leave Ethiopia in the 1970s?

4 What happened to the community in Gondar in 1984 and 1985?

5 What did Operation Solomon do?

WAR AND PEACE

A *"The world stands on three things – on justice, on truth and on peace."*

Ethics of the Fathers

As Jews meet one another and part, they say 'Shalom' [Peace] to each other. Jews have used this greeting from Biblical times in the hope that, one day, humankind really will live in peace with one another.

This does not mean, however, that most Jews are **pacifists**. Although war is always regarded as an evil, Jews believe there are times when it is right to fight.

OBLIGATORY AND OPTIONAL WARS

Judaism divides all wars into two groups:

Obligatory war:

There are many examples of this in the Jewish scriptures. After Moses died, for example, Joshua led the Jews into the Promised Land of Canaan. This land was not empty and the Jews had to fight to take it. It was God who commanded them to do this:

B *"...rise up, cross over this River Jordan... Every place where the sole of your foot treads I will give to you... be strong and courageous, for you will lead this people to take possession of the land which I have [promised to your ancestors]..."*

Joshua 1.2-6

This was an obligatory war – one that the Jews were commanded by God to fight. There are also three other kinds of war which Jews believe to be justified:

- A war in which a country is fighting in self-defence. Israelis would claim that the wars fought in the Middle East since 1967 have all been fought in self-defence.
- A war fought to help another country which has been attacked.
- A war in which another country is attacked because it is about to attack the Jews.

Optional wars:

This is a war that has a sound reason and every other course of action has been tried and failed. In Biblical times, hostile neighbours had been threatening Israel for three centuries by the time of King David. They had plundered, killed and taken captives. David attacked them and peace followed.

> ### TAKE TIME TO THINK
>
> Some Jewish parents do not allow their children to play with guns. Why do you think this is? When you are a parent, will you follow this course of action?

Jews believe that there are times when war is inevitable. Do you agree with them?

MARTYRDOM

Jews place a great emphasis on life but they accept that life must sometimes be set aside. This is martyrdom. Judaism expects Jews to surrender their lives rather than commit one of three sins:

- murder
- idolatry
- sexual immorality

Jewish leaders have disagreed over this. Some have believed that martyrdom is the final sacrifice a person can make for God. Others have taught that martyrdom serves no useful purpose.

OVER TO **YOU** ▶▶▶

Here are some Jewish teachings. What do you think they are saying about peace?

1 "Seek peace and run after it." [Psalm 34.15]
2 "Peace is the vessel for receiving God's blessing." [Mishnah]
3 "Peace is to the world what yeast is to dough." [Talmud]
4 "The Torah was given to establish peace." [Midrash]

PEACE

To Jews, peace is not a state which simply exists when people are not fighting one another. Peace is not just the absence of war. It only exists when people are in a state of friendship and co-operation with each other. It means that true harmony between nations makes fighting and war unthinkable. Such peace is a gift of God:

C *"And I will give peace to the land… so that the sword will not even pass through…"*

Leviticus 26.6

Jews believe that a time is coming when there will be peace over all the earth. This will happen when God sends his Messiah, who will set up God's kingdom on earth. When this happens:

D *"They will beat their swords into plough shares and their spears into pruning hooks, nation shall not lift up sword against nation nor shall they train for war any more."*

Isaiah 2.4

JUDAISM AND SCIENCE – FRIENDS OR ENEMIES?

You will find out

- Judaism has nothing to fear from science.

- The very important moral questions raised by religion.

- The ways in which Jews believe science should be used.

In the glossary

Rabbi

The 12th century Jewish thinker and rabbi, Moses Maimonides, left Jews many teachings that are still important today. It was Moses, for instance, who taught that there were the eight degrees of charity that we met in unit 25.

He taught that religion in general, and the Jewish religion in particular, had nothing to fear from science. The two are partners in humankind's search for the truth. In fact, science is a pathway to God since the more we study, and understand, about the natural world, the more we are amazed by the power and creativeness of God.

Whatever part of the human body we study, we are constantly amazed by what we find. This is true whether we are looking at the human eye, the ear, the heart, the joints and muscles of the arms and legs, or the brain. Only an all-powerful God, an intelligent designer, could have created something as complex as the human body.

NOTHING TO FEAR

Science has brought great benefits to humankind in the last 200 years:

CHECK IT OUT

Cures for diseases thought to be incurable.

Medicines which improve life for millions of people.

An understanding of DNA, which will lead to the curing of many current illnesses given time.

Some modern benefits of science

A greater understanding of the universe in which we live.

Gadgets which make life much easier.

Many prominent scientists have been Jewish. One such person is Dr Robert Winston, who is a world expert on human fertility. These people, and many others, have been sure that science does not present any kind of threat to the Jewish faith.

Yet science does confront us with many moral dilemmas which lead Jews to examine their faith very closely. Questions such as:

- Is it right to carry out an abortion and curtail a baby's life?
- Is it right to end a person's life early because they are suffering from an incurable disease?
- Is it right to commit acts of violence against other people knowing the terrible destruction that modern weapons can cause?
- Is it right to clone animals and so make it possible to cure many diseases in the future?

USING SCIENCE

Jews believe that God has chosen science to make known information about the universe, the world in which we live and all forms of life. Take an important example. The Jewish scriptures are quite clear that God created everything but they do not say anything about how this happened.

Jews, like everyone else, are curious to know how everything began. There is nothing in the search for answers that should disturb the religious faith of Jewish people. Neither the 'Big Bang' theory about the beginning of the universe or the evolution of all kinds of life challenge the Jewish belief in God.

Jews would insist that:

- **Life has purpose and meaning because that is the way that God created it.** Jews believe those who wish to know what that purpose is need to read their scriptures.
- **Human beings stand as the pinnacle of God's creation.** This is because they have been given a critical intelligence that marks them out as different to every other form of life. Humankind alone can discover God's secrets through scientific discovery and put those discoveries to the best possible use.

TAKE TIME TO THINK

In a world that is increasingly dominated by science, what important contribution do you think that religion in general, and Judaism in particular, can bring?

OVER TO **YOU** ▶▶▶

1 Do you think that Moses Maimonides was right? Is it true to say that the more we know about the world, the more we are amazed by the power of God?

2 What do you think are the three most amazing parts/organs of the human body? Do you think that only God could possibly have created them?

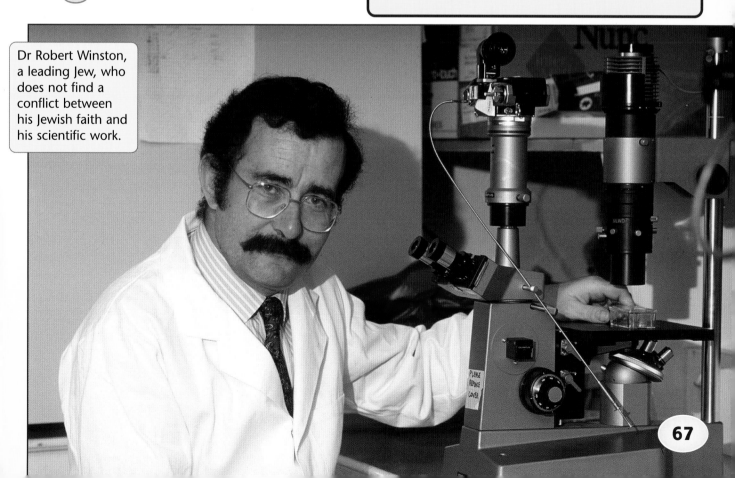

Dr Robert Winston, a leading Jew, who does not find a conflict between his Jewish faith and his scientific work.

Euthanasia refers to the ending of someone's life deliberately because they have an illness which is terminal and will shortly bring their life to an end. Judaism is strongly opposed to the idea of euthanasia. It uses the same texts from the scriptures to oppose euthanasia as it does to oppose abortion and suicide.

LIFE IS A GREAT BLESSING

Jews believe that life is the greatest blessing that God has given to the human race. As such, everything possible must be done to preserve it. There are 613 laws in the Torah which Jews have traditionally been encouraged to keep, but all but three of them can be broken if a person's life is in danger. Only three of them must be kept at all times and they are:

CHECK IT OUT

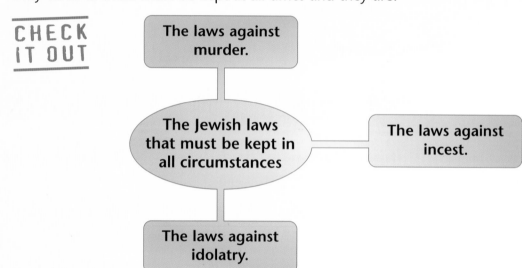

The Jewish laws that must be kept in all circumstances

- The laws against murder.
- The laws against incest.
- The laws against idolatry.

This shows how highly Jews value human life. The Jewish scriptures are very clear – it is God alone who decides when we are born and when we should die:

A *"Naked did I emerge from my mother's womb and naked shall I return there. The LORD has given and the LORD has taken away, blessed be the name of the LORD."*

Job 1.21

There is an old Jewish saying that three people are involved in the birth of every baby – the father, the mother and God. At the end of life, however, there are only two people involved – the dying person and his or her Maker, God. Euthanasia would be the same as playing God and that is completely unacceptable.

Judaism does not teach, however, that life must be preserved at all costs. It does allow a life-support machine to be turned off, for example, if someone is all but dead. Keeping a person alive artificially would also be against the will of God.

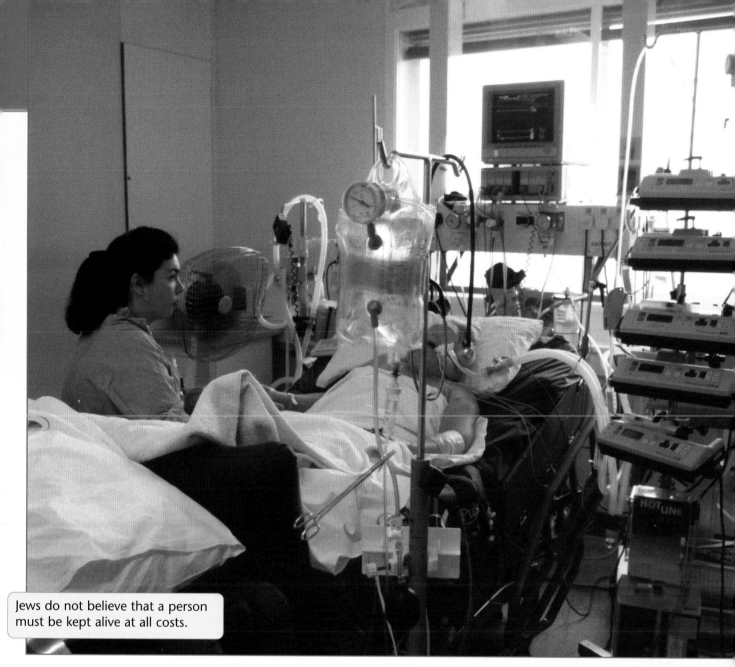

Jews do not believe that a person must be kept alive at all costs.

SUICIDE

As we have seen, believing that God is the creator of all life is a basic Jewish belief. So, too, is the belief that God gave human beings the right to make real decisions for themselves, but this does not extend to the right to take their own life [suicide]. Jews disagree with suicide, although they are usually very understanding about it. At this time, those who take their own life cannot have a normal Jewish burial or be buried close to other Jewish people.

TAKE TIME TO THINK

What do you think about the Jewish saying that three people are involved in the conception and birth of every baby, while only two people are involved in a person's death? Do you agree with it?

OVER TO **YOU** ▶▶▶

1   Explain to a friend what the teaching of Judaism is about the value of all human life.

2   How does Judaism show the great value that it places on human life?

3   What are the three things that a Jew cannot do – even to save human life? Do you think that there are any things which you would not be prepared to do to save a person's life?

GLOSSARY

Abraham: The father of the Jewish people, the patriarch who began the Jewish nation.

Anti-Semitism: Hatred that is directed against Jewish people because they are Jews.

Ark: The cupboard in the synagogue which houses the scrolls of the Torah.

Ashkenazim: Jews from eastern and central Europe.

Bar Mitzvah: Ceremony which marks a Jewish boy reaching adulthood on his 13th birthday.

Bat Hayil: The coming of age ceremony for girls at the age of 12 performed in Orthodox synagogues.

Bat Mitzvah: Ceremony held to mark a Jewish girl's entry into adulthood in Reform synagogues.

Bet Din: A court of three rabbis which pronounces on matters concerning the Jewish law.

Bimah: The bench in the synagogue on which the scroll is placed to be read during services.

Brit Milah: The Jewish ceremony of circumcision carried out on boys on their 8th day after birth.

Challah: Two loaves of white bread used during festivals and on the Sabbath day, over which the blessings and grace before meals are recited.

Chuppah: The canopy under which a Jewish wedding takes place.

Circumcision: The removal of the foreskin of a boy's penis on the 8th day after birth. Also called Brit Milah.

Diaspora: The dispersal of the Jews throughout many countries after the Romans conquered the city of Jerusalem in 70CE.

Euthanasia: The right, opposed by most Jews, for a person to end their life if they are suffering from an incurable disease.

Everlasting Light: The light that always burns above the Ark in a synagogue as a reminder that God is always with the Jews.

Exodus: The journey of the Jews out of Egyptian slavery towards the Promised Land of Israel.

Gentile: Someone who is not a Jew.

Get: The letter authorising a Jewish divorce.

Gospel: One of four books in the New Testament of the Christian Bible.

Havdalah: The ceremony held to close the Sabbath day in every Jewish home, marking a separation between the holy day and the days of work to follow.

Heaven: The home of God, the place to which all Jews hope to go after death.

Hell: A place of temporary separation from God, a place of preparation for heaven.

Holocaust: The murder of six million Jews by the Nazis before and during the Second World War.

Israel: The country which Jews believe has been given to them by God.

Ketubah: The marriage document that is signed by the groom before the ceremony takes place.

Kosher: Meat that is suitable for Jews to eat.

Menorah: The seven-branched candelabrum which is one of the most important symbols of Judaism.

Messiah: The Jewish leader sent by God to deliver Israel from all its enemies.

Mezuzah: Biblical texts inscribed on parchment in a small metal or plastic container placed on the doorpost of most rooms in a Jewish house.

Minyan: A minimum number of people, ten, required before a Jewish service can take place.

Mohel: Specially trained Jew who circumcises Jewish boys when they are eight days old.

Monotheist: Someone who believes in one God – Jews, Christians and Muslims are monotheists.

Moses: The leader who took the Jews to the edge of the Promised Land during the Exodus.

New Testament: The second half of the Christian Bible.

Onan: A Jew who has just lost a close relative and who is excused from all religious responsibilities for a short time.

Orthodox Jew: A Jew who follows all of the traditional teachings found in the Jewish scriptures, especially the Torah.

Pacifist: A person who does not believe in the use of violence in any situation.

Patriarch: A term covering the three Jewish 'father-figures' from the earliest days of Judaism – Abraham, Isaac and Jacob.

Pesach: The Jewish festival of Passover celebrating the delivery of the Jews from Egyptian slavery.

Prophet: A man or a woman who is sent by God to deliver a message to the Jewish people.

Pushkes: Boxes found in almost all Jewish homes to collect money for charity work.

Rabbi: 'Teacher', a person responsible for teaching and leading worship in a synagogue.

Reform Jew: A Jew who belongs to a group that does not keep all the old Jewish laws.

Rosh Hashanah: The Jewish New Year festival celebrating the creation of the world by God.

Sabbath Day: A day of rest for all Jews, celebrates the day that God 'rested' after spending six days creating the world.

Shechita: The only acceptable way to kill a kosher animal.

Secular Jew: A Jew who does not follow or celebrate any of the religious practices of Judaism.

Sefer Torah: The scroll of the Torah which is kept in the Ark.

Sephardim: Jews who originally came from Spain and Portugal.

Shavuot: The Jewish Feast of Weeks [Pentecost] celebrated fifty days after Pesach.

Shekinah: The presence of God, a word which indicates God's presence with the Jewish people.

Shema: The statement of belief taken from the Jewish scriptures, recited twice a day by Orthodox Jews.

Siddur: The Jewish prayer book.

Star of David: The six-pointed star, which is the most important symbol of Judaism.

Synagogue: 'Coming together', a place of prayer and worship for Jews, also used as a community centre.

Tallit: The Jewish prayer shawl of white material with fringes in which there is a blue thread.

Talmud: An important collection of Jewish law judgements from the past.

Tefillin: Two boxes containing quotations from the Jewish scriptures which are strapped to the forehead and left arm of Jewish men for prayer.

Temple: Magnificent building erected by Solomon in Jerusalem and finally destroyed by the Romans in 70CE.

Ten Commandments: The law code delivered by God to Moses on Mount Sinai.

Tenakh: The popular name for the Jewish scriptures – the Torah, the Prophets and the Writings.

Tithe: The Jewish obligation to give 1/10 of their income to God.

Torah: 'Law,' the word used to refer to the first five books in the Jewish scriptures – Genesis, Exodus, Leviticus, Deuteronomy and Numbers.

Treifah: Food that Jews are forbidden to eat.

Tzedaka: Word meaning 'justice' in the world.

Yad: The metal finger-pointer used by Jews to follow a passage in the Hebrew scriptures.

Yad Veshem: Memorial in Jerusalem to those who died during the Holocaust.

Yarmulke: Skull-cap worn by Jewish men in the synagogue.

Zionism: A group which fought for the right of Jews to return to their homeland of Israel in the 1930s and 1940s.